Speak Out:
Don't Freak Out

confident public performance

Ruth Bonetti

Published by:

PO Box 422,
The Gap Qld. 4061 Australia
Phone (+61) 07 3300 2286
Mobile (+61) 0411 782 404
http://www.ruthbonetti.com

First edition: 978-0-9578861-0-0 (2001)
Reprinted: 2001, 2002, 2004, 2005, 2007, 2009
Second edition ISBN: 978-0-9578861-3-1

This book is copyright. Apart from any fair dealing for the purposes of private study, research, criticism or review as permitted under the Copyright Act, no part of this book may be reproduced by any process without the written permission of the publisher.

National Library of Australia Cataloguing-in-Publication entry : (paperback)
Author: Bonetti, Ruth, author.
Title: Speak out - don't freak out : public speaking with confidence
          / by Ruth Bonetti.
Edition: 2nd edition.
ISBN: 9780957886131 (paperback)
Notes: Includes bibliographical references and index.
Subjects: Public speaking.
          Speech anxiety.
Dewey Number: 808.51

Cover: Sean Stanley (sean@maplekiwi.com)
Internal design: Book Whispers www.bookwhispers.net
Graphics: John Harrison
Printing: Lightning Source

Other books by Ruth Bonetti

Confident Music Performance: Fix the fear of facing an audience
ISBN: 978-0-9578861-6-2

Practice is a Dirty Word: How to Clean Up Your Act
ISBN: 978-0-9578861-5-5

Practice WAS a Dirty Word – Music Journal
ISBN: 978-0-9578861-2-4

Don't Freak Out – Speak Out
ISBN: 978-0-9578861-0-0

Enjoy Playing the Clarinet
ISBN: 978-0-19-322108-6

Enjoy Playing the Clarinet – Piano Accompaniments Book
ISBN 978-0-19-322109-3

Music Scales– Tips to make them happen (eBook)
ISBN: 978-0-9578861-1-7

Speak Out – Don't Freak Out (eBook)
ISBN: 978-0-9578861-3-1

Sounds and Souls – How Music Teachers Change Lives
ISBN: 978-0-9578861-8-6

Clarinet Series 2 (AMEB Grades 1-4, Allans Publishing)

Contents

Acknowledgments	vii
Introduction	1
Chapter 1	3
You are not alone	
Chapter 2	8
Taming the tremors	
Chapter 3	14
Brain, breath, body	
Chapter 4	32
Your voice is your instrument	
Chapter 5	43
As others see you	
Chapter 6	46
Preparing your speech	
Chapter 7	51
Countdown to performance	
Chapter 8	62
You're on!	
Further reading and bibliography	78
Index	80
About the author	84

Acknowledgments

Many thanks to all those who helped in various ways with feedback, advice, support, editing and technical and artistic aspects. Thank you Leonie McMahon, ASM, natural health practitioner, for input and for pointing me in the direction of a speaking career. Her expertise in the fields of alternative medicine, chiropractic, acupuncture and Applied Kinesiology has proved a very helpful contribution to this book. The late and missed Peter Egan, OAM, Estill voice consultant, directed me to recent research on voice production and breathing techniques and clarified the subtle differences in application by wind players, singers and speakers.

Particular thanks to my editor, Bob Johnson, for his superb knowledge of words and of the many processes required to contain them between covers, and to Rochelle Manners for the transition to eBook.

Introduction

It's normal to be nervous about speaking in public. In fact, fear of public speaking tops the list of the most common anxieties – including flying, dying and bankruptcy.

If people like Dustin Hoffman, Nicole Kidman and Peter Sellers admitted fear of live performance, why should we expect to be immune from freaking out when called upon to take centre stage? Sir Winston Churchill worried before his speeches. Martin Luther King was sleepless the night before his "I have a dream" oration.

We can experience nerves in different ways and need a smorgasbord of solutions to fortify ourselves for the varied symptoms and situations we encounter.

This book takes a holistic approach, offering practical advice to arm the presenter with ways to combat the wide range of challenges we face – to help us help ourselves.

It will show you how you can turn the fears and worries that beset the novice speaker into positives, which can free your imagination and empower your voice. You will learn that the panic that overwhelms us is, in fact, raw energy.

This book does not promise you will never feel nervous again. A little anxiety, anyway, will trigger your adrenaline to release that vitality, that charge of potent electricity, so necessary for communication on-stage. Rather, you will learn how to channel the adrenaline rush and turn it to positive use, and how to manage and alleviate the unsettling symptoms that make public speakers tremble.

Then you can anticipate, utilise, and even welcome the adrenaline rush as a source of power to lift your presentation from the merely mundane to an exciting and enriching performance.

You will take centre-stage with confidence and enjoy the art of communication.

Chapter 1

You are not alone

Fear of public speaking is as old as Moses and as topical as Jerry Seinfeld. It is a fear that tops dread of flying, dying and bankruptcy. As Seinfeld says, "At a funeral you're better off in the coffin than giving the eulogy".

With any public speaking it is normal to be nervous sometimes. For some speakers, this is part of the thrill as the adrenaline starts pumping. For others, it's all a fog, and the mind goes blank, as blank as a crashed computer screen.

Maybe you can relate to all this? You are on stage, totally exposed to row upon row of uplifted, squinting eyes of the audience who are staring … waiting … expecting …

You wrench dry lips apart, force out that quavering first word. It stumbles, stutters and your frail confidence shrivels up like something nasty in the bottom of the refrigerator. Your speech skids downhill. Your thoughts tangle like spaghetti.

This book will help you learn ways to rise to the challenge of public speaking instead of inwardly dying a thousand deaths through your nerves.

Perhaps you think you are alone in your misery. Most sufferers of stage fright nurse their nerves as an embarrassing dark secret, imagining they alone experience them. They are afraid to admit their fears in case they appear incompetent.

The first thing to understand is that it is okay to be nervous and you're normal if at some time you tremble while speaking in public.

Nerves have inhibited most presenters at some time or other; many top speakers have been paralysed by them at times. It is often the highly creative, thoughtful performers who suffer the most while matter of fact people may appear to cope better. The very depth, imagination and sensitivity which enriches exceptional speeches often takes a toll on those who conceive them.

Sadly, many with significant speaking ability never realise their full potential because of nerves. Their vivid imaginations, capable of drawing out the sublime, can also predict numerous mishaps and stumbles, turning the minutes, hours, days, or weeks before a presentation into miseries of imaginings – many unlikely to eventuate.

To all of you who suffer from such agonies, take heart. You suffer because you are not a potato. Does a potato possess your abilities, your sensitivity, or richness of imagination? Do you want to present like a potato? Do people pay to hear potatoes speak? Your imagination makes your life harder but, when you have conquered your fears, it will set you apart.

Perhaps the first recorded instance of "presentation anxiety" occurred around 1300BC when God commissioned Moses to urge Pharaoh to free the Hebrew slaves. "Why me?" pleaded Moses to God. "I am a nobody. I am not eloquent. I am slow of speech and slow of tongue."

Poor Moses. As well as having to argue with God and Pharaoh – and convince the Hebrews they should follow him to the Promised Land – he had to overcome his insecurity as a speaker.

To this day, the same insecurities have beset many famous people until they conquered their nerves.

Sir Winston Churchill was so nervous of a fledgling speech in the House of Commons that he fainted – yet he went on to become a respected orator.

Actor Sir Laurence Olivier described his temporary phase of panic as "a catatonic state of gut-rotting terror".

Actor-politician Glenda Jackson, winner of two Oscar awards, spoke of dreading the butterflies that invaded her stomach from late afternoon on performance days. By early evening, her palms sweated and fingers shook as she sat down to do her makeup. Before curtain-up, with heart palpitations, she feared she simply couldn't go on.

All these people – and they are only a few examples – have suffered, and conquered, the fear of going before the public. We commonly call it stage fright.

How did these troupers conquer their stage fright? They just kept on facing their audiences.

Experience breeds confidence

It is far harder to stoke yourself up for occasional presentations than to face regular ones that become routine.

Forcing yourself into frequent performance opportunities develops confidence born from experience, and the knowledge that "Hey, I survived! I got to the end! I did it!"

So how did Moses fare? God convinced him he could do it. Moses fronted Pharaoh, at first politely (and nervously) with a respectful "please let my people go". But with each meeting he grew more bold and confident until he thundered that God's wrath would descend on Egypt.

Moses' story reveals an important truth – the more we speak in public, the less our fears intrude and the more we grow in confidence.

If Moses, the self-confessed "nobody", could surmount his fears, so too can we.

The No.1 phobia

The *Book of Lists* reported that fear of public speaking is the number one phobia in the United States, ahead of flying, dying and bankruptcy.

A Canadian study (reported in *Psychology Today*, May-June 1996) found a third of Winnipeg residents reported excessive anxiety when speaking to audiences.

Their major concerns were:
1. 80% – trembles and shakes.
2. 74% – fear of their mind going blank.
3. 64% – doing something embarrassing.
4. 63% – being unable to continue.
5. 59% – saying foolish things, or not making sense.

Some things to understand about stage fright
- It is no respecter of persons.
- Anyone can experience it at some time in his or her career.
- There are no haves and have-nots.
- It is not a personality trait or mental disorder, but a response to a pressured situation.
- The degree of anxiety is not related to the level of the person's ability – or lack of it.

So why do we feel so bad?

Many speakers and performers mistake normal tension for nerves. Heightened senses and feelings are natural when on stage. If we don't feel this excitement, we should not be there!

Without this adrenaline rush, a presentation is likely to be matter-of-fact and boring. We simply need to learn how to turn it to positive use.

Many less experienced speakers are alarmed by the tension that floods their bodies, but it can be channelled for powerful delivery.

Compare this with electricity. If we harness it, we have great resources of power available.

If we fight the waves when surfing, we will struggle, swallow saltwater, and probably be roughly dumped. But ... wait for the next wave, watch it build up, catch it on the crest, go with it, and allow its power to sweep us along. Frightening? No. Exhilarating!

Chapter 2

Taming the tremors

The symptoms which afflict all performers, particularly public speakers, we will call the "Top Ten Tremors". The anxiety which has been building up as the time of a public speech approaches is hit by the adrenaline rush in the moments before you take centre stage, causing you to feel like you are losing the plot.

Tick the "tremors" listed below which you have experienced:
1: Wobbly knees, fidgets, shaky hands
2: Brain fog, memory lapses
3: Gasping for breath; short of air
4: Trembling, shrill, nasal, rushed or husky voice
5: Queasy stomach
6: Excessive perspiration and flushed face
7: Dry mouth, tight or ticklish throat
8: Shoulder, neck or back ache
9: Panic attacks
10: Frequent visits to the bathroom

How did you rate? If you ticked:
0-1 – Impressive! (Are you real? Or in denial?)

2-5 – You're normal.

6-10 – You're still normal, and there are solutions.

The root of the problem

"I'm flushed, sweaty, and I can't hear myself think – or speak!" How often is this your feeling when you have to stand up and speak?

Many novice public speakers struggle with shakes, dry mouth, hoarse or ticklish throat, blocked brain. Their voices, delivered with cotton-wool tongues, sound wooden, dull monotones. Or they burst out with over-loud braying, giggling at their own jokes which fall inert into a leaden silence. They gabble, stammer. Sentences are littered with "um" and "er". They are tongue-tied, confused and inhibited. What they planned to be an expressive flow is little more than a sludgy quagmire.

Even before their event tension escalates. In sleepless nights, fitful restless dozing merely reveals worst fears in nightmares. By day, they are overtired, irritable, can't concentrate. In the countdown to the presentation, they haunt the bathroom with a queasy stomach or diarrhoea. On the launch pad backstage, they fidget, pace and shake.

Why do we suffer so? The answer is that all these symptoms are part of the fight or flight reaction to fear. And they're as old as primitive man.

Imagine Fred Flintstone toasting a chunk of mammoth over the fire in his cave. He sees glinting through the flames the eyes of a sabre-toothed tiger. In a matter of seconds more than a thousand reactions charge through his body. His heart races, pumping blood to his vital organs, strength to his arms and legs. This gives him incredible power to either grab his children and sprint, or to attack the tiger with his bare hands and fling it into the fire. This is the adrenaline rush which mobilises us for action and survival.

These powerful physiological changes are designed to protect us – from our own sabre-toothed tigers there in the front row – just as they have preserved the human race for millennia. Unfortunately such reactions overwhelm the unprepared. Then they seem to work against us instead of for us.

At the mere thought of a threatening situation, our body prepares to fight or flee, so that:
- The body's heart rate, and hence blood pressure, increases.
- Blood pumps urgently towards our brain, to maximise clarity of thought, and towards our muscles, to steel them for action.
- Simultaneously blood is pumped away from the digestive system, to conserve energy.

How does this translate for the public speaker?

As our hearts beat faster, blood rushes to the brain and so it is not surprising that our face becomes flushed. But why do we simultaneously feel hot and yet have sweaty, clammy hands? Because the body in its wisdom has built in an air-conditioning system to cool down contracted muscles and protect delicate organs from the heat of increased blood flow!

Often our pounding heart seems so loud that we fear that the audience won't hear our presentation.

When Meryl Streep accepted an Oscar for *Kramer vs. Kramer* she confessed she couldn't hear what she was saying because her heart beat so loud. As our innate sense of tempo is measured relative to our heart beat, it is not surprising that we tend to rush when under pressure. This increased heart rate and brain activity – things seem to happen quickly around us – combine to create confusion and overwhelm us. "I just can't think straight," we say.

Our body reacts to protect us from our particular tigers; we instinctively contract and tighten our shoulders into a hunched posture. Our neck muscles pull our head down and shoulders up. Our breathing becomes shallow and gaspy.

These adrenaline reactions are normal, in-built instincts geared to keep the human race intact by maximising strength and focus. They are a healthy response as long as you do not remain in a state of tension for prolonged periods or become overwhelmed by an excess of adrenaline.

The public speaker is likely to experience some, perhaps even many, of these *natural* fight or flight reactions. The secret of success on your feet is to anticipate these reactions, understand them and turn them to your advantage.

Fear

Fear can be a useful emotion when it causes us to protect ourselves, to take care, to avert catastrophe or problems. Normal fear, in reasonable proportions, is useful as it motivates us to take precautions and even lifesaving actions. If we fear an armed robber we can take sensible precautions like double-locked doors and burglar alarms to ensure better sleep.

Thus, a manageable degree of fear is valid, even helpful. Extremes manifest as panic (a sudden surge of acute fear) and irrational anxiety, when we act as if we were under great stress although there may be no apparent cause. Discuss these with a mentor, or a professional counsellor who may help with relaxation techniques, biofeedback, meditation, behavioural therapy, hypnosis and other techniques.

Anxiety

On the other hand, anxiety is a vague, nebulous, all-pervading malaise, in which we feel continually threatened but with no definite cause. We are bedevilled by lurking worries, which have no names, or specific sources.

These may build into a paralysing state of "high anxiety." If you feel an overwhelming sense of panic or worry but there is no specific fear causing it, seek help from some form of counselling.

A most important initial step is to face, confront and admit our fears. Free flow of expression is blocked if we do not do so.

Many hope to jolly themselves out of their morass, to think away or throw off their fears: like the ostrich, they bury their heads in the sand until problems seem to just go away. Of course this is hardly a comfortable presentation posture, besides limiting projection.

Keep your sense of humour

There is real power in a smile or a laugh.

When paralysed with nerves, we need to keep a sense of humour. Buddha said: "Nothing is left to you at this moment but to have a good laugh."

Ancient Chinese medical texts vouch for the healing effects of laughter. A physician in Classical Rome noted that women who were "melancholy" were more likely to have "tumours in the breast".

"A cheerful heart is a good medicine, but a downcast spirit dries up the bones," says the *Book of Proverbs.*

Being gloomy is hard work! We use 13 muscles to smile, but 72 to frown.

Laughter is a powerful medicine. When Norman Cousins, author of *Anatomy of an Illness,* was diagnosed with severe spinal arthritis, doctors gave him a one in 500 chance to live. He noticed that the pain lessened when he laughed. Along with other therapies, such as intravenous doses of vitamin C, he watched comedy videos, thought positively – and laughed his way to health.

Smiling is even a brain-tonic! For when we smile, our facial muscles contract, sending increased blood to our brain. With increased blood flow, the brain receives an oxygen bath similar to that from a short exercise workout.

Enjoy your gift, your opportunity to present, and your audience will respond positively.

Chapter 3

Brain, breath, body

Most presenters have at some time encountered that nagging little voice that lurks in vulnerable and pressured minds. Like a doom and gloom revivalist preacher it predicts disasters out of minor hitches. It speaks with such conviction that who are we to dispute it? Dispute it we must. Such thoughts sabotage our success.

The American anthropologist Margaret Mead estimated that the average human utilises only four percent of his or her potential. Recent studies put this as low as one percent. How much of that wastage is because our brains are clogged up with negative thoughts and worries! Truly, as Buddha said: "We are what we think. With our thoughts we make our world."

The Greek philosopher Aristotle said: "What you expect, that you shall find." The Roman philosopher Marcus Aurelius said: "Our life is what our thoughts make it." The Stoic philosopher Epictetus wrote: "Men feel disturbed, not by things, but by the views they take of them." In more modern times, the noted American motivational lecturer Norman Vincent Peale said: "You are not what you think you are, but what you think, you are." Henry Ford summed it up as "Whether you believe you can or can not – you are right." Virgil wrote: "They can because they think they can."

Ironically, many battle against a crippling fear of failure only to discover that success is equally challenging for they must live up to an even higher yardstick. Dustin Hoffman's biographer noted that, he had first gone to his psychotherapist because he felt he was a failure and also later he needed help to cope with success.

To try to understand the problems we face with public speaking, let us consider the three Bs – Brain, Breath, and Body.

Solutions for public speaking anxiety begin at the top – with our brain. When we feel threatened in an exposed situation, such as standing up to speak to a crowd, the primitive section of the brain takes over. This resembles that of reptiles, to whom survival, a speedy escape from danger, strength, and the quick strike are basic. As our body revs up to meet challenges this "reptilian" brain-stem response speeds our heartbeat and contracts all the muscles of our body in preparation for the fight or flight, affecting our breathing, equilibrium and muscle tone.

At the same time, the more sophisticated part of the brain, the cerebral cortex, with which we reason, think and speak, seems to shut down, overwhelmed by the reptilian brain. As blood is directed away from the brain to the lungs, arms and legs, we say: "I just couldn't think straight".

We need to:
- Slow down internally, deliberately curbing the primitive responses.
- Systematically condition ourselves to deal with such pressures.
- Breathe in and out slowly.

- Place a hand on our forehead for a few moments.

This eases butterflies in the stomach, un-blocks "brain-fog", releases the memory box and curbs excess fight or flight impulses so a new response to the situation can be learned.

Probably instinctively you have used this technique, but you didn't realise its potential. Remember when someone fired a question, you put your hand to your forehead, saying "I know this… it's on the tip of my tongue…"

What happens is that blood flows to the frontal lobes behind the forehead, where rational thought occurs. These are the emotional stress-release neurovascular balance points for the "stomach meridian" of ancient Chinese medicine, named Positive Points in Brain Gym (see below), a form of Applied Kinesiology. Both Western and Eastern medical authorities recognise the need to keep the electromagnetic circuits of the body (described as meridians in the Chinese system of acupuncture) flowing freely.

The power of the whole brain

It is normal that people favour one brain hemisphere at the expense of the other. Presentation stress increases this natural inclination. Those who are predominantly "left-brained" may become too obsessed with fine detail and analysis, losing the "big-picture". Or "right-brained" speakers may be flighty, easily distracted, wrestling to contain an unfocused "butterfly brain." They need a proportion of left-brain sequence and analysis.

Much of the preparation of a speech focuses on left-brain information and facts. It is important to balance this with the realisation that audiences' brains tend to focus on right-brained aspects like our body language, rhythm of speech, vocal timbre and imagery. We are more effective speakers if we can balance our logic and analysis with colourful imagery and expression.

Educational Kinesiology or Edu.K. (derived from the Greek root *kinesis*, meaning motion) is a personal development program of human body movement, pioneered by educator and author Paul E. Dennison and his wife, Gail Dennison. Their program, Brain-Gym, develops brain-body wholeness with simple movements like cross-crawl (i.e. crossing over the mid-line between brain hemispheres) which enable people to access parts of the brain previously inaccessible to them.

Originally conceived to correct learning disabilities, this wholebrain learning is used by people from many fields (professionals, students, athletes, dancers, musicians, artists) to draw out their hidden potential and to make it readily available.

Some over-diligent people, by trying too hard, "switch off" the brain-integration mechanisms necessary for complete learning. Thus, information that is received by the back brain as an "impress" is inaccessible to the front brain as an "express". This inability to express what is learned or to stay "centred" locks us into a failure syndrome, resulting in irrational fear, flight-or-fight reactions and frozen emotions.

Brain-Gym exercises can make radical improvements in the learning stages of preparation. Various exercises improve facility of a wide range of everyday experiences, relating to effective functioning of both sides of the brain. Even a simple action like the steepling of fingertips balances and connects the two brain hemispheres. Many exercises are directly relevant to projection, resonance and focus in stage performance.

Of these, the "PACE" (Positive-Active-Centred-Energy) fourstep warm-up sequence helps poise and concentration both in practice phases and presentation.

1. The first step is simply to drink water. As a marathon runner, Dr Dennison learned the many benefits of water. A dehydrated performer's responses become sluggish as the electrical and chemical actions of the brain and the central nervous system are conducted by fluid. This is especially relevant for the speaker whose voice and

system need hydration of at least eight glasses of water per day – even more in periods of stress.
2. Massage the soft tissue under your collarbone, while holding the navel with the other hand. Among other benefits, this activates the brain to send messages from the its right hemisphere to the left side of the body and vice versa, facilitates the flow of electromagnetic energy and increases the blood supply to the brain. It frees the public speaker's ability to cross the visual midline and thus keep his or her place while reading and to blend consonants.
3. Cross-Crawl, or cross-lateral walking in place, involves alternately moving one arm and the opposite leg and then the other arm and leg, such as when we march. This accesses both brain hemispheres simultaneously and is an ideal warm-up to improve co-ordination, breathing and stamina, to enhance hearing and vision.
4. The final steps, called Hook-Ups, connect the electrical circuits in the body. First cross one ankle over the other, whichever feels most comfortable. The hands are then crossed, clasped and inverted. A simple and unobtrusive method to do this back-stage is to cross one arm over the other, opposite to the legs. If your left ankle crosses the right, then the right arm should cross the left. Rest your tongue behind your upper teeth while inhaling slowly. Continue breathing out and in for a few minutes.

This exercise decreases adrenaline production by bringing attention to the motor cortex of both frontal hemispheres, away from the brain stem's survival mode. The mind and body become more flexible as energy circulates through areas blocked by tension. The figure of eight pattern of connected arms and legs follows the energy flow lines of the body.

The PACE exercises are invaluable for emotional centring, for balance and co-ordination, deeper respiration and for releasing emotional stress, especially before meeting a challenge such as a presentation.

Kinesiology has a holistic approach that deals with the physical, chemical, emotional and spiritual aspects of a person's neurological health. It discovers areas of nerve interference and offers solutions and appropriate treatment. It can clear focus and become a form of preventive medicine, leading to better health by improving the immune system and increasing the ability to focus and to cope with stress.

Many presenters are blocked by suppressed memories from childhood. Perhaps a teacher or parent made some unthinkingly cruel comment like "Sit down and be quiet. You haven't anything worthwhile to say!" American therapist Stanley Keleman says the adult speaker may unconsciously carry deep inhibitions as a result of such stored "insults" or physical and psychological trauma. The muscles remain "on guard," protecting from issues which reverberate to this "memory in the muscles," thus restricting free action of the voice and body. Indian-American doctor and pioneer of alternative medicine Depak Chopra has extended this concept to cellular memories.

Health practitioners such as chiropractors and osteopaths, through Applied Kinesiology's Neuro Emotional Technique sessions, may release such "insults" and memories. Muscle testing shows where areas of nerve interference occur and how it creates disorganisation within the nervous system. Simple treatment can bring immediate results. (This author can attest that such treatment broke a long-standing pattern of "switching off" caused by a combination of negative thought patterns, food intolerances and hurtful memories such as nicknames and childhood taunts.)

Brain Gym and Applied Kinesiology are holistic and "whole-istic", a powerful means to free the psyche and allow the voice to speak out with confidence.

Combat self-sabotage by acknowledging anxieties and negative feelings, but framed by these empowering words: "Even though I ... I love and appreciate and respect myself." Reinforce this by tapping on meridian points to short-circuit emotional and thought blockages, as directed in the accessible Emotional Freedom Technique. (http://www.emofree.com/)

Breath, the basis of life

Just as our breath is the very basis of life, so it is the lifeblood of all performance. Significantly, the word "inspiration" relates to breathing, our very life force. For without breath, what are we? Breathing is central to all performance. It is essential that speakers are aware of and draw on this vital resource. Amplifiers can pick up shallow breaths in audible, irritating gasps. Deeper breathing is subtle, fuller and provides resonance for the voice.

Air is still free! We can use as much as we need, even waste it, without concern or guilt. It is when we hoard our air or forget to release it, that we panic, fearing that we don't have enough, and so we often do run short. A major problem when we are under pressure is that we forget to take time for a good deep breath between sections. Just as a car cannot run without petrol, so a speaker cannot produce rich vocal resonance without adequate air.

Yet it is possible to create further tension by trying too hard with breathing. Having overheard my decades of teaching clarinet students how to breathe correctly, my three sons asked me to check their own breathing. Because they tried too hard, each one in turn demonstrated exactly how not to breathe. When we are relaxed, breathing is a natural, easy process. However it is precisely because we are not relaxed onstage that we need to explore correct technique.

When we feel threatened, the contraction of our muscles inhibits natural breath flow. As part of the fight or flight reaction, when pressured we all tend to hold our breath. This tenses our bodies ready for action. Performers who forget to release their air and inhale find themselves trapped in ramrod, frozen postures. Prolonged breath holding causes insufficient oxygen flow to the brain and thus a lower energy level.

Breathing is an involuntary action that has functioned without conscious direction since our birth. Watch a pet or baby sleeping. See the movement as their ribs expand, their chest rises and falls as they breathe. We are astounded that a baby's small lungs can produce such an incredible volume of sound. This is because infants breathe naturally and easily and use their whole chest, diaphragm and lung mechanism. Speakers should also use this capacity.

For the speaker, the major vocal issue is not lack of air, or the necessity to inhale enormous amounts. The amount of air required to project to the back of an auditorium is relatively similar to that of normal speech. What is needed to reach the back of the room is more sound energy, rather than just air volume. In fact, taking a huge intake may cause breathy tone, because the air will want to rush out. Or, when tense, we may inhale air but forget to use it!

The root of the problem for speakers is tension, specifically that of the vocal folds. Our "true" vocal folds and lungs are protected from

HOW THE DIAPHRAGM WORKS

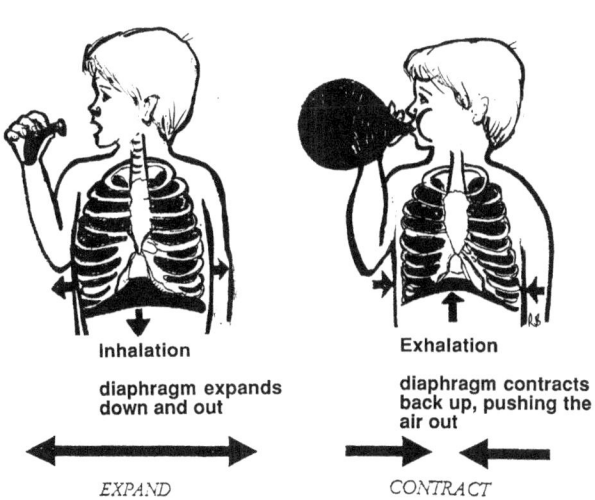

Inhalation
diaphragm expands down and out
EXPAND

Exhalation
diaphragm contracts back up, pushing the air out
CONTRACT

food ingested the wrong way, or from an insect straying inside, by the involuntary closing of the "false" vocal folds. When the fight or flight reaction causes all our muscles to tense, inevitably our voice is choked because the false vocal folds clamp shut. Notice your natural reaction to close your false vocal folds if you clench your fist hard and grunt.

Open these false vocal folds with Santa-type "ho ho ho" or by a big belly laugh or a sob. (It is not surprising that operatic singers produce round, resonant tones as they constantly express such extremes of emotions!)

On-stage, we can discreetly replicate this action silently to release false vocal folds locked by fear. That's all the more reason to include healthy humour and laughter in your speeches. This retraction of the folds produces a richer vocal timbre and allows projection over a wide range without strain.

The speaker's voice is a meld of three main components – the lungs (the powerhouse), the voice box (the source of sound) and the throat-mouth-nose vocal cavities (the resonating chamber). An easy flow of air through this pipeline from deep in the lungs produces a smooth stream of well-modulated words without tensing the throat and jaw.

Singers talk of drawing up the air from their feet to remind themselves to breathe deeply using the diaphragm, that network of largely involuntary muscles which divides your lungs from your stomach. The following natural activities show how we already use our diaphragms in everyday living. Locate your diaphragm by placing your hand just above your navel. Pretend to smell a beautiful rose or lavender, fake a cough, yawn or sneeze, or call out "Boo!" and you will feel your diaphragm at work. Or light a candle, blow steadily so that the flame tilts, then blow it out.

Inhale, sounding "eeek" ... then compare another inhalation saying "ohhh" as in "hot." Notice that the former felt shallow, tight, unsatisfying and the latter quick, deep, easy, lasted longer? A dome shape openness inside your mouth also aids retraction of the false vocal folds.

Notice your breathing patterns while lying relaxed, perhaps drowsing in bed before sleeping. Lie comfortably, with the knees bent, a hand above your navel. Empty your lungs with a gusty, audible sigh. Let it go freely; don't force it. Release all that stale air which has sunk to the bottom of your lungs. Give an extra huff ... imagine the tide drawing out to sea. Wait a few seconds until you really need a breath, then it will flow naturally, instinctively. It will be deep and satisfying ... and correct.

Having emptied the lungs first, you will breathe deeply, correctly, without any conscious thought. The lower chest area will lift, then the upper chest – this latter is not a "no-no", after all, we do have lungs enclosed in there! As you breathe out, notice that your lower chest subsides first, then the upper chest.

Another way to identify correct action is to place your hands over your lower ribs at the side. Gently ease out the air. Feel the ribs and lower back muscles expand as you inhale. Or make a diamond shape by meeting both index fingers and long fingers placed just above your navel. As you breathe in your fingers should separate, then meet as you exhale.

Regular exercise, such as swimming, aerobics or walking, is a pleasant way to develop lung capacity. For those who prefer breathing "exercises" and especially to relax before a presentation:

Lie down and relax. Slowly exhale fully, wait, then inhale and hold. Breathe out ... give a huff at the end ... wait ... breathe in ...hold a few seconds ... inhale ... repeat. You will find that your capacity and consequent counting increases over a period of time.

Many are surprised at their increased capacity when they discover their "back-expansion breathing". As our chests accommodate our heart and other organs, our lungs stretch wider at the back. To locate this extra resource, sit, bend forward, head towards your knees, fingertips at either side of your backbone. Feel the expansion as you inhale.

In delivery, some speakers experience a pent-up feeling of "not having enough air". They desperately snatch frequent shallow breaths, hyperventilate and become clogged up with too much air which they don't take time to exhale. This can cause light-headedness and fainting.

Although we tend to breathe in through the mouth when needing quick, full intake, it is preferable to inhale through the nose where possible. This has the added advantage that less noise is picked up by amplification. Slow inhalations are more soothing, whereas constant quick gasps may add to our feeling of unease. The reality is that in a presentation we hesitate to take time to exhale, or for a deep, slow breath. Yet, listeners do appreciate "catch-up" time to absorb your content. You can gain time for this by asking a question and using the answers to breathe, or by walking across the platform.

Experienced speakers pace themselves and ensure that they always inhale adequate breath. It does help to plan this by speaking through your material well before the event, choosing breathing places between sections. Mark these with a symbol such as // or pencil "OUT" for exhalations between sections. Notice your natural pacing, rhythms and patterns in everyday situations; how long you pause between sentences; observe how you instinctively phrase, pace and breathe. Yogis have discovered that deep breathing relaxes the body and mind. They use it as a path to meditation, relaxation and general health.

So, you are about to go on stage. You are energised. You feel a bracing in the torso with ribs working freely and breath coming easily. You are prepared to deliver your message with a resonant and confident voice.

Body posture

The speaker's instrument is the body – all of it, from the toes up. Not just the mouth that moves. Breathing is closely linked with good posture – and to our fears. Let us go back to that basic fight or flight reaction to fear. When threatened by that sabre-toothed tiger we instinctively protect ourselves with hunched shoulders, thus constricting and shortening our spine and squashing the muscles required for efficient air intake.

Audiences are quick to read body language, absorbing far more from this than from actual verbal content. Research has shown 55 percent of your presentation's impact is determined by your posture, gestures and eye contact, 38 percent by your voice, tone and inflection and a mere 7 percent by your content. The audience tends to focus far more on the speaker's body language, rhythm and imagery than on the actual words. For example, folded arms are a sure signal of an insecure or defensive speaker.

Poor posture robs the speaker of conviction as well as resonance. A slumped posture is not a compelling look, hardly persuasive to the listeners. It can cause restricted breathing and a dull, nasal voice because the rib cage constricts the lungs.

Slumped stance constricts breathing, voice loses resonance

Such poor posture and repeated body misuse can damage the voice as Australian actor Frederick Matthias Alexander discovered early last century. His recurrent loss of voice during performances threatened his career.

Alexander spent desperate hours in front of a mirror, observing the muscles used in speech. He noted breathing interference and some curious movements of his head and neck, not only when he spoke but even when he merely thought of performing. When he learned to use his body correctly his voice problems ceased. His Alexander Technique evolved into a system of therapy which focuses awareness on body usage, balance and posture. It is based on the premise that use affects functioning. It is a relaxed system of non-doing and awareness rather than busy exercises.

A major focus of the Alexander Technique is on restoring the natural habit of stretching and lengthening our spine, freeing and opening out our bodies. We reconsider how we move through everyday actions so that the head leads the body.

Thus, we are uplifted and harmonised in an efficient blend of balance, effort and subsequent relaxation and breathing. Mental directions to the crucial muscles and body parts achieve a sense of "up-ness" to counteract gravity's compression. When bad postural habits are eliminated, the back widens and the spine lengthens, the neck "lets go" of tension.

Correct, comfortable posture allows us to move easily, freely and to project positively.

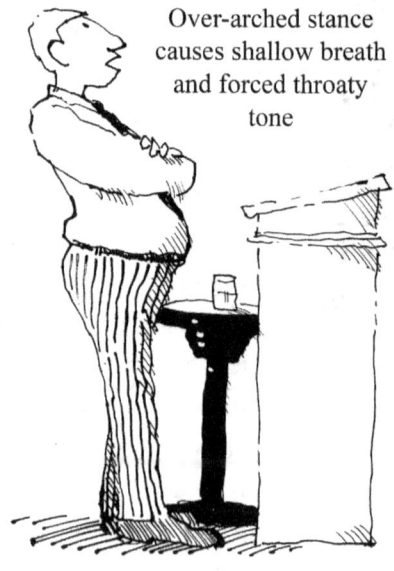

Over-arched stance causes shallow breath and forced throaty tone

What is "correct" posture? At the very word people instinctively over-compensate into a rigid parody. In a forced attempt to achieve "correct" posture, overarching the back risks backache. This tightens our abdominal muscles and locks our knees, causing tension through the body. Many stressed people have almost perpetually locked knees, lower back and neck. The fight or flight reflex triggers the "tendon guard reflex" which shortens the calf muscles and locks the backs of the knees so the body, to align and maintain balance, moves forward onto the toes. Neurophysiologist Carla Hannaford believes this postural problem is a major cause of inability to speak freely. Prolonged use of a rigid stance can even make presenters feel dizzy or faint.

The ideal position should be comfortable and natural. Expand your chest while lifting high the back of your head. This lengthens your spine so you stand tall like a puppet on a string.

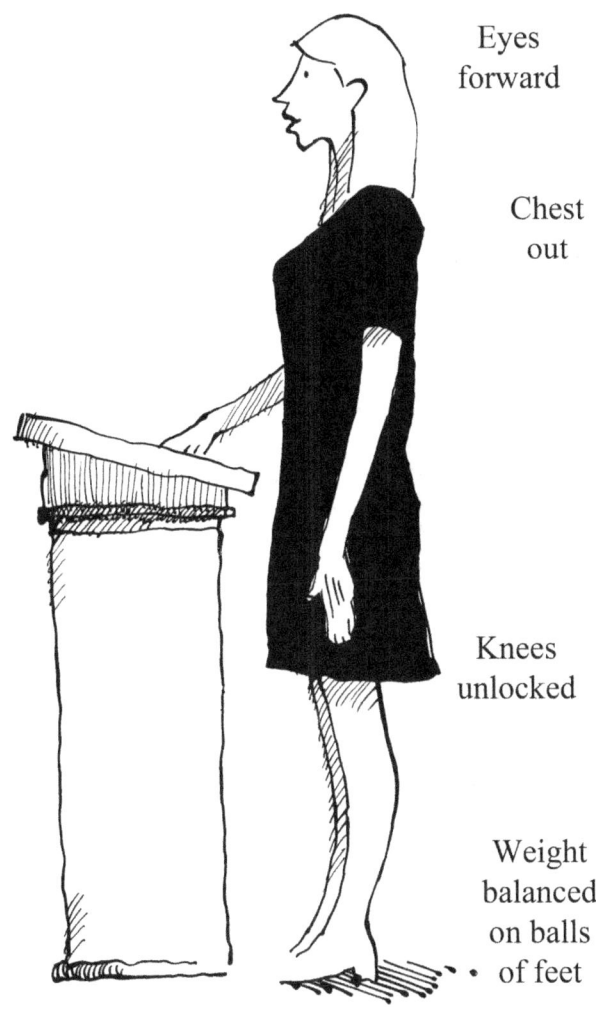

To find this natural, comfortable balance, stand with your back to a wall with head and feet slightly away from it. Lightly press the torso, from shoulders to buttocks, against the wall as much as possible, given the inherent S-bend of the spine. Bend your knees slightly, thus unlocking their tension, and tuck your tummy into that "bikini-girl" posture, which in turn tilts your pelvis forward a little. Do you notice how your chest has expanded out into that Pavarotti type pose common to good singers?

Chin too high causes voice to sound strained

Probably this seems forced and unnatural, but it looks poised and confident. Stand against the wall for a few moments periodically to accustom yourself to this posture. Make it a habit. Speak a few words and you will hear improved projection, depth and quality of your voice. Common postural habits like leaning to one side, overstrained upward chin or lowered chin can distort your voice production. They cramp and inhibit the lungs and larynx (although trained actors and singers manage to produce full resonance in a variety of unnatural postures!).

A positive natural posture is relaxed but upright with the chin up, the chest out and the back straight. Make your spine taller. Imagine your ears are pulling you upright! Press your heels into the floor, balance equally on both feet.

Your back will straighten, your chest will expand and your voice will project with ease and resonance at its natural pitch
.

Chin lowered causes husky, rough voice, restricts projection

Diet

As athletes maintain a carefully balanced diet regimen, so should all performers. Especially, what can we eat before a presentation to access the required energy? When the fight or flight reaction activates, blood is directed away from the digestive system. Eating a big steak just before a presentation will only make us feel sluggish and sleepy, because the task of digesting animal fat draws oxygen from the body tissues.

Experts suggest eating five or six small protein meals a day as this is less likely to cause a hypoglycaemic attack when blood sugars drop after a large meal. A small, healthy snack about two hours before speaking maintains steady, optimum blood sugar levels and sustained release energy. Complex carbohydrates such as bread, potato, rice, whole grains and legumes, eggs, pasta or oatmeal biscuits, which contain fibre, are easily digested. Plan ahead to eat most protein at breakfast and opt for lighter forms like fish, chicken or eggs closer to the event.

If you cannot face eating, suck glucose lozenges or drink Glucodin to keep up your energy levels. Fresh fruit juices are easily digested but avoid acidic citrus. Grape juice gives quick energy, relieves nervous exhaustion and clears phlegm. Avoid dairy products, which increase mucus, and oily or fatty food.

Performance stress causes dehydration. During challenging times, increase water intake to improve concentration, mental and physical co-ordination; it alleviates mental fatigue, increases energy levels, and relaxes for improved communication. Our bodies are made up of about 70 percent water, which is an excellent conductor of electrical energy, necessary to efficiently pass messages between the central nervous system, brain and sensory organs. Water is best consumed at room temperature or even warm. Iced water should be avoided for the body must warm this before it can be absorbed into the system; cold constricts the throat whereas heat relaxes it.

Another source of fluid is herbal tea such as peppermint (eases digestive upsets), sage (a tonic for brain and nerves), chamomile and valerian (reduce nerves and insomnia), St John's Wort (an antidepressant for mild anxiety and excitability), maté (a general tonic for exhaustion and tiredness) and catmint, thyme and valerian, which calm the nervous system.

Chapter 4

Your voice is your instrument

"There is no index of character so sure as the voice," said former British Prime Minister Benjamin Disraeli. Even the most interesting, erudite material can bounce away from listeners' ears if delivered in a nasal, strident, hoarse, thin, breathy, dull or sarcastic voice.

Indira Ghandi was tongue-tied, inarticulate and squeaky in the early stages of her prime-ministership, yet she became a fluent, fiery debater.

Margaret Thatcher's original Lincolnshire accent and affected, often shrill voice spelt electoral disaster until she worked with a drama coach who slowed her speed and lowered the pitch of her voice by forty-six hertz which is half the difference in pitch between the average male and female voices.

Grace Kelly's high nasal voice was honed into a lower, sexier pitch by a drama coach.

Michelle Pfeiffer's plain natural speaking voice proved an asset because it could be more easily coached and modified into various accents or dialects.

We are all capable of modulating and changing voice qualities:

many have done so unconsciously, picking up inflections from a partner, roommate or by moving to a different area or country. We can radically improve poor vocal timbre and increase range with conscious thought and listening.

Varied modulation and pitch range enhance presentation but listeners tend to sleep through dull monotones. They would have difficulty sleeping through a newborn baby's range of up to five octaves! Well-modulated speaking voices use a pitch range of around 8-10 notes. Female voices are about an octave higher than males.

Pitch is determined by the number of vibrations per second of your vocal folds as measured in hertz, with lower voices moving at fewer hertz (around 130 cycles a second) and high ones ranging up to 1397 for a soprano's top "E". Tension, the primary enemy of good voice production, also tightens and lifts timbre.

As we face an audience full of "sabre-toothed tigers", instinctively we tighten all muscles defensively. As our vocal folds, throat, jaw and larynx tense, our voice becomes thin and lacking in authority, a telltale sign of nerves out of control – or insecurity may be expressed in frequent rising inflexions like question marks. This "up-talk" is known as high rising tone. If you notice this happening as you speak, rather than inwardly berate yourself, simply bring the voice lower at the end of the next sentence. You have turned a negative into a positive by increasing your vocal range.

Some tense speakers may be disconcerted that their voice seems to shut down. When they open their mouths to speak they produce a mere croak. This is caused by tension and fight-or-flight syndrome; the false vocal folds, designed to protect us from choking if we accidentally swallow a fly, clamp shut. Open this mechanism with a discreet social yawn before beginning to speak.

A rich and positive voice is more pleasant to the ear and conveys credibility. Society tends to respect a lower voice as one having an air of authority. Unfortunately, some actors have actually damaged their voices in an effort to lower their voices – an effect that can be obtained with ease by retraction of the vocal folds.

Women who have high pitched and thin sounding "little girl" voices can be trained to lower their pitch by learning to consciously retract the false folds (remember the feeling in the larynx when you laughed or sobbed silently), thus producing a more authoritative sound. The pitch only needs to be reduced by a few hertz. Even a semi-tone will be useful. Experiment by reading stories to small children and dramatise them using different character voices. You can train your voice to a lower pitch with no damage to the true vocal folds as long as you remember to keep the false folds retracted.

Before walking on-stage, find your natural range by making a surprised "oh, oh" type sound (as in "hot"). To reassure yourself that your voice is working freely, make a sound like a siren over about one and a half octaves. Intone "he he he, ha ha ha, ho ho ho". Plant a supportive partner or colleague in the audience to tip you off with a subtle gesture if you are speaking too fast, high, loud or soft.

A truly nasal voice is one where the opening from the throat to the nasal passages fails to close on all vowel sounds. Only three sounds should pass through your nose – m, n and ng. You can improve your voice quality by making sure you get a full closure of this opening to the nose by making a hard "G" sound saying "hung-gee, hung-gair, hung-gah, hung-oh, hung-gu".

As a warm-up, yawn with the teeth and mouth fairly closed and round your lips as if saying "oo", "one" or "open".

Speech projection, enunciation and facial expression require a flexible jaw and this also helps to prevent constriction of the false folds. As 50 per cent of brain signals pass into the body through a junction box at the jaw, called the temporomandibular joint, all areas will function more efficiently if locked jaws are freed.

This can be done best by wiggling your jaw loosely from side to side and massaging the hinge of your jaw, just in front of the ear. If you feel an urge to yawn, let it happen – this is one of nature's best remedies for releasing tension and increasing oxygen intake.

A yawn and a good stretch are great stimulants because they can:
- Release toxins and waste material in the blood.
- Causes a strong downward movement of the diaphragm.
- Stimulate a full intake of air.
- Release stiff trunk muscles caused by tiredness.
- Improve circulation to the head.
- Relax tension in the jaw, throat and face muscles.
- Improve voice quality.

Voice resonance may also be improved with a Brain Gym exercise called "thinking caps" which is done by unrolling the curved rim of your outer ears several times. This relaxes the jaw, tongue and facial muscles.

It also:
- Activates the brain to help you hear with both ears.
- Screens out distracting sounds from relevant ones.
- Switches on reticula formation and helps listening comprehension.
- Helps public speaking, singing, playing a musical instrument.
- Helps short-term working memory and thinking skills.

Poor articulation results from tense jaw, lips, palate and tongue. Improve this with silent laughs and yawning and massage the TMJ (temporomandibular joint). Blow raspberries. Roll your Rs. Relax the tongue by exploring your teeth and gums with it. Warm up facial muscles by acting out a wide variety of emotions. Pull funny faces. Gently nod from side to side. Walk around breathing and stretching. Open your mouth sufficiently to articulate without mumbling!

When former US president Bill Clinton suffered hoarseness, talkback lines ran hot as many people related that they had also experienced similar problems in their speaking. Suddenly, the topic came out of the closet.

Speakers need to take care of their tools of trade – their voices. Just as an athlete would never compete without thorough physical and mental warm-ups, it is vital for speakers to prepare themselves.

Physical loosening and limbering unwinds tension and induces deep breathing. This can include stretching, yawns, yoga exercises and Tai Chi.

Vocal warm-ups

As you've been making sounds all your life you really need very little effort to warm up the vocal apparatus. The only warm-up you really need is to make a sound like a siren on an "ng" as in "sing", throughout your range. This needs to be a small sound achieved by effort in the large muscles of the neck and torso with only a little air being used. (Prove how little air is needed by sirening silently! Make sure you use the same effort in the same muscles as when you made sound. This is also the time to pay attention to retraction of the false vocal fold as the aim is to wake up all the muscles involved in producing sound.) The silent siren is particularly beneficial to help maintain vocal flexibility during a performance in those times you may be actually off-stage or in the wings.

Other actions you may find useful are gentle humming in a comfortable mid-range (e.g. "ohhh" as if expressing mild surprise) of easy small range tunes like *Three Blind Mice* or *Frère Jacques*. When the voice is flowing, expand the pitch range progressively higher and lower. Always use a most comfortable vocal effort in making a sound. Softer sounds, paradoxically, need more effort.

Buzz your lips as you hum to limber up your lips. Make "brr" motorbike sounds.

Open up the throat by saying "aah" as you do when you go to the doctor.

Or say "ohh" while you bend your knees slightly, feet flat on the floor. Bending your knees prevents their locking, which can cause tense stomach and glottis muscles and thus a throaty tone.

Say the alphabet interspersed with the word "awesome" while maintaining the same pitch: "awesome-a-awesome-b-awesome-c-awesome-d" and so on. Feel the openness at the back of the throat – the retraction.

Or say the *Hot Potato*: "One potato, two potato, three potato, four; five potato, six potato, seven potato, more." Imagine eating a too-hot potato. This really opens – retracts – the throat.

Breathing warm-ups

Feel a satisfying movement of an expanded and flexible rib cage with these exercises:

- Blow a sheet of paper against the wall with a steady stream of air; or blow a candle (good for volume control).
- Laugh or sob (encourages retraction of the false folds).
- Take a breath and exhale on "fff".
- Hiss. Make mosquito-buzzing noises.
- Hum. Vocalise on "meow" so all the vowels are activated.
- Yawn, sigh.

The voice under pressure

Our old bogey, tension, is a major cause of vocal problems. Constricted vocal folds rob voices of resonance and projection and can lead to vocal trauma.

The efforts required to contend with problems such as background noise, insufficient or no amplification, or unreceptive audiences (such as in classrooms and lecture theatres) can strain the voice. A solution is to use a technique called oral "twang" or "safe yelling". To do this take a short, high breath, brace your torso, retract the false folds and make spontaneous loud sounds. Practise the happy yell of Italian mamas when they call out for the children and papa to come for dinner – "mangiamo!" … let us eat. Another example of the spontaneous "yell" is the cry made by a baby moments after birth. Or a child's "Muuuum".

Can you recall a noisy party where there is usually one voice that can be heard over all the rest? What a loud voice, you think. What's more, that kind of voice quality never seems to tire. The difference is the amount of "twang" or "ringing" quality in the voice, a sound made by tightening the collar of the laryngeal tube, which creates another resonator within the vocal tract. The extra resonance in the 2 to 4 kilohertz band of the sound spectrum contributes to the perception of loudness or "ringing" tone.

To protect your voice in noisy environments you need to activate this twang quality to enable you to be heard more easily without vocal trauma.

Seminar leaders, schoolteachers and lecturers, who handle large and sometimes unruly groups, can avoid yelling by using techniques such as "room ecology" where the speaker defines his or her expectations of the audience. Actors and experienced speakers know to stand centre-stage forward for their strongest message and move to the side for a more relaxed or lighter effect. Similarly, teachers and lecturers can establish their expectation of attention by moving closer to the audience – or even amongst them. They will quieten and listen, allowing the speaker to use normal voice levels.

When speaking in the open air, use an acoustic hailer. Stand in front of a wall to enhance the sound. In outdoor work, be careful to keep warm. When shivering with cold, we tend to tense up our neck, shoulders and rib cage and tighten our joints, leading to constriction of the false vocal folds and poor vocal performance. Remember to retract. A few drops of eucalyptus oil on a tissue inside a shirt pocket or bra will help this retraction.

When contending with environmental risk factors – such as dust, smoke, chemical pollutants and a dry atmosphere – you should increase water intake to hydrate the vocal folds. Aircraft travel combines the noise and dryness issues, so keep speech to a minimum when flying. Coughs and colds can be catastrophic for anyone whose employment requires constant voice use, whether as a speaker, actor, teacher, lecturer, singer, or media presenter. Problems are exacerbated if halls, studios and classrooms are poorly ventilated or centrally heated, with the resultant dry air affecting the vocal folds.

Solutions for vocal problems

If you strain your voice, check if it was caused by constricted false vocal folds, in which case silent laughs, sobs and sirening may help.

Also:
- Increase water intake. Borrow the singer's maxim, "pee pale, speak clear".
- Rehydrate the vocal folds with steam inhalations and a humidifier.
- Use lozenges such as Fisherman's Friend, or those containing zinc, slippery elm, ginseng or Echinacea. Avoid analgesic lozenges.
- Essential oils such as eucalyptus, lavender and frankincense may be inhaled with steam.
- Honey soothes the throat. Paul Newman said he drank a couple of jiggers of honey for his energy and for his throat before a stage performance.
- Drinks of warm honey and lemon soothe and heal. Gargling lemon kills germs in the throat. Increase

vitamin C supplements, but ease off if diarrhoea indicates overdose.
- Humidify your bedroom or work environment, especially during winter.
- Maintain good health through exercise and adequate, balanced diet.

Laryngitis (inflammation of the larynx) responds to hydration, riboflavin, niacin and zinc supplements. It is most essential to rest if you are unwell. Keep germs to yourself; go to bed and recover as quickly as possible. Medical treatments may include aspirin, cough suppressants and decongestants (but avoid antihistamines). Gargle with warm water and salt. Naturopathic gargles, including sage, horehound or slippery elm, can help.

Natural remedies include eating garlic (a natural antibiotic) and ginseng. Gargling tea-tree oil can prevent a sore throat developing into full-scale infection. (The author has successfully used it internally in small doses of three drops in half a glass of water up to three times a day for one or two days. Be warned, however, that it is classified as a poison.)

Don't:
- Speak if you have a cold or laryngitis, or if it hurts to swallow.
- Speak consistently too high or low.
- Overtax a voice in fragile condition or try to "speak through" flu, sore throat, hoarseness or fever. (A fatigued body is a risk to your voice.)

Beware of:
- Mucus-producing foods (dairy products, chocolate) especially before presenting. Also nuts, which could catch in the throat.
- Smoking (including passive smoking), alcohol, caffeine and drugs.

Alcohol depletes the body of B vitamins and magnesium that combat tension. The depressive effects of alcohol can be exacerbated by hot stage lights and overheated rooms so you feel more flushed and uncomfortable. Excess alcohol, especially of spirits, raises body temperature and increases blood flow to the vocal folds, causing possible damage and roughening voice timbre.

Caffeine lifts blood pressure, increases the heart rate, can constrict the blood vessels and causes increased urination and gastric secretions. It may trigger anxiety disorders. Chocolate, some analgesics, flu and sinus medications and pharmaceutical stimulants may contain caffeine.

A natural remedy for a stuffy nose is to irrigate warm salty water through the nostrils into the sinuses, inelegantly known as "sniff'n'spit". This circumvents nasal drip and throat irritations.

As well as illicit drugs such as cocaine and marijuana, beware of using beta-blockers and stimulants. Beta-blockers are prescription drugs that block the adrenaline reaction; they do not stop nerves, but they lessen their anxiety symptoms. They lower the heart rate, reduce sweating and tremors and alleviate a dry mouth or jitters. Potential side effects can include triggering asthma, cardiac conditions, anxiety or mental illness, dizziness, light-headedness, nightmares, hallucination, lethargy, insomnia, visual disturbances, diarrhoea, loss of appetite, cold hands and feet, loss of hair.

Also be cautious of medications that dry the throat such as antihistamines, corticosteroids, anti-inflammatory drugs and anaesthetic throat sprays.

Carry throat lozenges to secrete in your cheek if you develop a ticklish cough. If your voice wavers or cracks this may be due to constricted air supply. Take time for a deep breath and a sip of water before proceeding. Tense neck muscles can be eased with massage, subtle stretches and yawns.

Seek medical advice if throat problems continue as constriction may cause nodules. Chronic hoarseness or a "lump in the throat" sensation may be a result of common reflux laryngitis (gastro-oesophageal reflux). Vocal polyps, ulcers or nodules result from voice abuses, such as prolonged constriction of the vocal folds, yelling, or projecting out of range, without that open laugh, sob or siren sensation. Rest and implementing correct usage solve most problems and the vocal muscle is quite forgiving of minor strain. However, if chronic hoarseness continues it is wise to consult an ENT specialist, as sometimes an injury requires surgery.

Looking after your voice ensures you are equipped to take the stage and deliver your message with projection, poise and confidence.

Chapter 5

As others see you

Stage presentation is often forgotten or underrated by novice speakers, but professional poise can be as memorable as the content of your performance. Unconsciously, people assess you just as much by your manner and body language as by the actual performance. Give-away signs of nerves can be curtailed by awareness. The hands are the greatest culprits, prone to flapping, fluttering, clenching or stabbing at the air. They should be kept low so they will not upstage your face. If really necessary, curb their restlessness behind your body or loosely by your side – but avoid your pockets!

Make gestures that are relaxed, natural, relevant, definite and varied. They should be timed exactly to the point, or slightly preceding it. Poor timing gives a "canned" artificial look. A large auditorium needs bigger movements because subtle facial or hand movements will be lost.

Your image

Dress is important, not just for the look of it but because it increases your own confidence and poise, and makes you feel and look special.

It is safest to err on the side of over-dressing rather than under-dressing. But don't go to fussy or outrageous extremes. Aim for understated elegance. Be aware of current fashion but resist the bizarre. Simple, stylish clothing presents best.

Know the dress conventions of your particular field. For example, academics at conferences tend not to overdress, with even the top people in the field favouring smart casual. If presenting at a conference, bring a choice of outfits and observe colleagues before deciding.

What matters most is good grooming, from neat hair to polished shoes. Face and hands are focal points and so need special attention. Clothes should be clean and freshly pressed. Wrinkle-free fabrics stand up to the rigours of travel.

Women tend to dress "up" more than do men. Resist excessively high-heeled shoes, glamorous as they may look, which can cause foot cramps, as well as upsetting your posture. Check new shoes for slippery soles, and take the precaution of rubbing them over a rough surface like cement before the performance.

Choose colours and styles to enhance rather than detract. Shirts and blouses should be lighter than jackets. Colours should be middle tones, pastels (which may appear as off-white in spotlights or on TV). Bright red can show you up in a neon glow. Stark white can upstage your face and eyes by their appearing brighter.

For television, avoid garish patterns, which will distract from your face. Choose subtle rather than bold patterns. Avoid plaid, herringbone, stripe or checked patterns, which might appear to ripple or vibrate on the screen. Grey or brown eye shadow usually enhances eyes, but avoid electric blues or greens, which may give a ghostly look. Avoid jangly or shiny jewellery that will pick up distracting reflections. Even for radio interviews, you will gain confidence by knowing that you look your best.

Distracting mannerisms

Embarrassed gestures, nervous twitches, tics and stutters signal nerves. We may be painfully aware of some mannerisms; others we disbelieve until we see a video replay. How often do we see speakers slipping glasses on and off their noses, cleaning them, fiddling with them? Simply print out notes in a type large enough to dispense with the glasses altogether.

Clear pockets of coins and keys beforehand to reduce irritating jingling. Foil rocking body movements by keeping your weight firmly on the balls of your feet. Avoid unnecessary movements – aren't we irritated by speakers who wave and stab at the air? Gestures of the arms and face are preferable to big body movements, giving a more vital impression.

Before the big day, dress in the outfit you intend to wear and practise your speech and stage deportment. Work with a mirror or video camera and seek the advice of a mentor or colleague. Treat it as a real performance, gearing yourself through the day, quietening yourself and focusing.

All these suggestions will help your image, but the most important thing to do is be as natural as possible, believe in yourself and be yourself.

Chapter 6

Preparing your speech

Did you call, sir?" called the valet to Sir Winston Churchill, who was soaking in his bath.

"No, I was just giving a speech to the House of Commons" came the reply. Churchill, an inspiring orator, was said to spend an hour's preparation for each minute of a speech. One of his secretaries wrote

that, "Quick as was his wit and unfailing his gift for repartee, he was not a man to depart from the theme or indeed the very words that he had laboriously conceived in set-speech form. To the last he retained a sense of apprehension in addressing the House of Commons, or, for that matter, any large assembly." (from *Sayings of the Century*, by Nigel Rees, Allen and Unwin, 1984)

Research and write out your speech exactly as you would deliver it, whether you choose to read it, to learn it by heart, to speak impromptu with outlines on palm-cards, or use a prepared text with main points highlighted by fluorescent pens or red-ink points marked in the margin. Your choice will depend on your preferred manner of projecting your own personality.

Writing your speech

An Irish politician described his system of giving speeches: "First you tell them what you're going to say. Then tell them. And then tell them what you have told them." A good speech needs a beginning, a middle section or body and a conclusion.

Know your audience. Check beforehand with the organisers as to venue, guest list, demography, and expectations.

Know your topic! Research. Choose active verbs in short sentences, clear grammar. Keep it simple. Remember, your speech is intended for listeners' ears, not for their eyes. Speak it out aloud while writing.

Audiences appreciate an overview, to keep them on track: "I will tackle this question from three angles, namely ... to prove that ..." Mark off these points clearly, to shepherd wandering thoughts back onto the trail. Use pointers such as "Let me emphasise ... "or "The important point is ..."

Divide your speech into point form, clearly marked by numbers and use memorable sub titles. Plan how you will capture your listeners' attention by changing the timbre or speed of your voice, directing a question, showing visuals or moving across the stage.

To read or not to read

Fortunately, reading of speeches seems to be confined to the territory of formal academics. Audiences certainly respond better to a pair of eyes, however nervous, than the speaker's bent head.

There are some situations where reading is advisable for part or all of a speech. These include:
- When you must avoid misquoting or misinterpreting, e.g. with a press release about a sensitive issue.
- For accurate technical equations and complex calculations.
- When you must synchronise with another person who operates transparencies or a teleprompter. Rehearse together first.

If you do read:
- Maintain eye contact as much as possible (scan sections of your notes and look up to deliver – a lowered chin constricts the voice).
- Keep sentences short.
- Use wide margins for notes, signals to "pause" or "smile".
- Use clear point form and highlight headings.

To memorise or not to memorise

Certainly, memorise, if you have a photographic memory! However, most of us who don't would feel even more nervous of mental blocks. Sir Winston Churchill's memory failed once in Parliament and he subsided, head in hands. He apparently learned from this lesson; there are various accounts of the time he spent preparing speeches and a friend commented: "Winston spent the best years of his life writing impromptu speeches." He also perfected a trick to inject the impression of the impromptu into read speeches. He wrote into the text signals to pause, as if searching, before producing that telling word.

A compromise to memorising the whole speech is to:
- Jot down the points you intend to make.

- Speak freely into a tape recorder.
- Type up the words into a full speech. Polish it.
- Attack the speech with different coloured highlighters according to your category codes.
- Transfer onto medium sized cards the key words. of each section, in point form, and quotes or figures which must be exact. Cards are more discreet, do not crackle as paper does.

Packing your briefcase

Now you've prepared your speech and you're ready for the big event. As well as the text of your speech (how many people have turned up without their notes?) your briefcase could contain:

- A bottle of filtered water; most of your water intake will be en route to the presentation rather than when on-stage (where that jug may contain iced water, courtesy of ill-advised organisers!)
- Eucalyptus drops or cough lozenges especially those which contain honey and Echinacea.
- Homeopathic or flower remedy drops – Dr Bach Rescue Remedy.
- A multi-vitamin supplement or vitamin B such as Berocca.
- Lemon and ginger or other herbal tea bags.
- Liquid saliva spray.

- A spare pair of stockings/tights/hose for ladies. For men, a spare tie, cufflinks.

Chapter 7

Countdown to performance

A first response from performers asked "How do you prevent stage fright?" was "Prepare! Practise! Thoroughly and with plenty of lead time."

We do reap what we sow. If we know, submerged deep down under the procrastinations, avoidances, excuses and distracting trivia, that we have neglected solid preparation, some nerves are as inevitable as applause follows a class act. However, performance fears are surely lessened when we have prepared securely and wisely in the weeks and days before the event.

We can program our brains like a computer, feeding in correct information as to the sequence of words, sections. Then, if a blur of panic overwhelms us in the initial moments of a presentation, we can safely go into "auto-drive" for a few moments, knowing that our brain is securely programmed and will send messages to lips without our consciously driving them. Herein lies confidence. Yet, if in the initial preparation stages we have not logically thought through the basic arguments of our speech, such weaknesses will surface when we deliver under stress.

Fail to prepare > prepare to fail

Program your dreams. See yourself succeeding. An important part of the build-up to a performance is the mental preparation. Sit or lie comfortably relaxed and undisturbed while you visualise yourself sailing successfully through the speech.

See yourself, calm and poised, walking onto the platform, opening your mouth to speak. Hear the vibrant tone that flows out. Out of the corner of your eye, see those fear-gremlins skulk away into the shadows at the back of the stage, while you are encompassed in the warm, flattering and protective stage light.

Do you notice how the faces in the audience respond to you, smile up at you? Hear them clapping, shouting "Bravo!" See yourself backstage with diary open, wondering where you can find time for a repeat presentation.

Create a self-fulfilling prophecy. If you can see yourself in this positive light, you are well on the way to fulfilling all your hopes and dreams.

Repeat positive affirmations to yourself. Some possibilities are:

"It is all right that I allow myself to feel nervous, vulnerable, or fearful. I ask for the help and support that I need."

"I allow myself to enjoy this presentation, mistakes and all."

"I accept that my best is good enough."

"I strive for excellence rather than perfection."

"I allow myself to make mistakes, and I keep going."

"I am glad to have this opportunity to learn through any mishaps."

"What a great opportunity to present tonight."

This mental preparation will help overcome the common tendency to self-sabotage. When you hear those little negative voices run riot in your head, here's what you can do:

- Acknowledge and confront them.
- Mentally turn down their volume.
- Block them with proactive positive thoughts like: "I think I can".

- Use positive affirmations such as "I know I can".
- Blot out the thoughts with a meaningless chant like "blah blah blah".
- Try a Shakespearian touch with "Out, vile thought!" or just say "STOP!"
- Recall in your mind the words of people who have encouraged you.
- Use an icon: put a can of bug-spray nearby and use it as a reminder to conquer the "thought-bugs".
- Test yourself against the "thinking distortions that hamper": tunnel vision, too-rigid control, thinking the worst, blaming others.
- Be strong. Ban such over-generalisations and negatives from your mind:
- Terrible ("It's all terrible!")
- Awful, poor.
- Everybody, none, nobody. ("Everybody says …")
- Always, never.
- Ought to ("orta"), should have ("shoulda").

Replace them with flexible thinking:

"Sometimes I stutter, but mostly I speak clearly."

"Usually I prepare well."

"In some cases I stumble, but only slightly."

Negatives become less of an issue if we focus outwards. Be passionate about your subject. Love your audience.

The effects of "nerves"

Many performers notice that nerves increase the frequency of urination. To reduce the need to urinate immediately before a performance drink your water earlier in the day and just sip before and while speaking.

Pre-performance qualms can also trigger diarrhoea. Try Gastrolite or an equivalent over-the-counter remedy from a pharmacy. If you use a prescription drug such as Imodium, it must be taken about two and a half hours before performing because it may cause dry mouth, drowsiness or fatigue. An old remedy is a few sips of brandy.

Help for "nerves" may be found with flower remedies such as Doctor Bach's Rescue Remedy, gelsemium or homeopathic ipecac (note that the medical form of ipecac induces vomiting). Dr Bach's Rescue Remedy helps presenters to centre and to alleviate panic, exhaustion, tiredness and fear.

Australian actor Sigrid Thornton, popular star of the ABC's *Sea Change*, returned to the stage after spending the past 20 years in front of the camera. She admitted to some opening night nerves: "I'll be using a little bit of Rescue Remedy on the tongue." (*The Australian*, 27 February, 2001).

Ginger is excellent for calming upset stomachs and is often included in travel motion remedies. Drink lemon and ginger tea or infuse grated fresh ginger in hot water.

Some people prevent nausea and travel sickness by wearing acupressure magnets on elastic wristbands. This is applicable to stomach nerves in performance. Relief can be felt by massaging or pressing on the pressure point (called Neigun, or PC6) that is located about two fingerbreadths above the wrist crease, between the two main tendons on the inner forearm. Press firmly or stroke towards the wrist. This pressure point is also useful for treating shortness of breath, insomnia and anxiety.

Massaging the sensitive area 5cm around the navel (the adrenal points) can relieve emotional stress. Holding the forehead can release tension of the stomach.

Dry mouth, that bane of performers, is exacerbated by throat tension. To relieve it:
- Relax your throat by dropping your jaw and rubbing the underside of your tongue against the inside of your teeth. This activates the lubricating saliva glands.

- Press the tip of your tongue on the hard palate near the teeth ridge.
- Subtle sucking movements promote saliva.
- Imagine the taste of lemon juice or vinegar.
- Simulate yawns.
- Bite on your tongue.

Rather than drinking water immediately before your performance, rinse your mouth or gargle with warm water (warmth relaxes the throat and vocal cords). Drink sweetened tea with milk or suck a boiled sweet, cough lozenge or slice of lemon to increase saliva. Chew sugarless gum or smell some vinegar – its aroma prompts saliva. Simulated yawning also stimulates salivary glands. Check if your medications may worsen the problem. A pharmacist can supply an over-the-counter spray solution that creates artificial saliva. The yoga "lion" pose, with tongue outstretched, also promotes saliva, while relieving tension.

The days before

Plan the lead-up days, rescheduling where possible other tiring commitments like meetings to lighten your workload. Organise equipment, clothes.

Maintain a balanced, healthy diet. Curb caffeine, alcohol, nicotine, and drugs. Double your water intake. Spend time in mental preparation; see yourself succeeding.

If possible, rehearse in the venue to become accustomed to the acoustics and feel of the hall. Make allowance that an empty hall is more resonant than one filled with people. Ask a colleague to listen to this rehearsal to give an objective appraisal of volume and pitch, to check whether your voice projects to the back of the hall.

The hours before

Don't feel guilty about being as lazy as possible on the day of a big challenge as long as a sensible routine is maintained. We can all learn from actors and singers who know to "save themselves" as well as their voices on the day of a performance. They talk less, eat less, pamper themselves a little, and don't rush around. They retreat into themselves, focus on their part or persona, and especially avoid arguments or upsets.

Tension is energy that is blocked. Release it in whichever way works best for you. Go for a run, or other exercise. Many find they perform well if just slightly physically tired. It is often helpful to offload jitters caused by the excess adrenaline charge.

A long soak in the bath is wonderfully relaxing, even more so with various herbal oils or mineral salts. Water is a well-known therapy proved from Roman times. Even a five-minute bath or a quick hot shower unravels muscle tension. Massage shoulders, arms, back of neck. Stretch, yawn.

Eat a light snack (e.g. rice, pasta, bread), maintain water intake, rest, meditate or pray and mentally prepare. Visualise yourself succeeding.

Plan to arrive at the venue in good time without rushing. Get used to the space. This will allow you to check for problems or obstacles to a smooth performance, such as an electrical cord that might set your entrance off to a flying start. How close is the drop down to the stalls? Check that tapes or video illustrations are rewound ready at the correct point. Test overhead projection, PowerPoint slides, video and sound systems. Fiddling with equipment as you speak does not build confidence or credibility. Nor does pressing the reverse button on the slide projector.

Are the audience's seats so distant you must roar? If so, ask to move the podium or the chairs closer. Is the lectern so high that you would peer over it? Or so low that you can barely see your notes? For a more professional entrance, leave your papers on the lectern beforehand, especially if you are the first speaker.

Give a typed introductory biography to the presenter to read as your introduction. Ask for whatever you need. A jug of water? (Remember that stress dehydrates.) Better lighting?

Ask a colleague or recording technician to check microphones and sound levels. How close should you stand to the microphone so all "p" sounds don't explode like popcorn cooking? Will your voice fade if you move to the side of the lectern? If you walk around the stage with a radio microphone, will some areas attract reverberations or feedback?

Author and former ABC radio presenter Sandy McCutcheon described how he arrived at a speaking engagement to find no podium and no lighting: "I intended to read notes so I wanted light. And I wanted a podium, because otherwise it looks tacky and I don't feel comfortable without a podium. If I don't have anywhere to put my hands they may shake like crazy. Because, of course, there is nervousness, although I enjoy the nerves."

McCutcheon said he liked to get used to the space. "I like to look round the room, feel comfortable with it, know if there are possible distractions – like, if there is a window behind you, ask them to put a curtain over it so the focus will stay with you."

As you approach the last half-hour before going on stage, sit quietly and read through your notes.

The half-hour before

Now is the time to do those things that can avoid distraction or embarrassment – such as discarding jangly jewellery, keys, coins and turning off your mobile phone!

Protect your space. With tensions running high backstage, it is easy to become tangled in other people's traumas. During a preparation we all need space for centring energies, calming thoughts and for mental preparation. Everyone develops personal rituals of preparation, and just as we hope others will respect our space before launching out into the footlights, so we must be considerate of their need for privacy, even in crowded dressing rooms. Relaxation techniques are ideal here for calming and for general wellbeing. But do not expect to be relaxed on stage – there, tension is inevitable and can be harnessed into vital energy. You shouldn't try to be hyper-relaxed – you need to inject a manageable amount of tension to power your delivery.

Make time to get yourself mentally focused for the task ahead. Open your brain with the PACE sequence, especially the kinaesthetic "cross-crawl" exercises for easy access between the right and left sides of the brain.

Don't curb the instinctive tendency to pace the floor. Walking is a natural, easy form of cross-crawl. Movement keeps blood flowing, delivering more oxygen to the heart and brain. It also prevents the blood from pooling in your feet and is a positive way to unlock your brainpower.

At this time, the dreaded fidgets can arrive. Curb them by steepling the hands with fingers pressed together – a technique which also balances the brain hemispheres.

Another easy hand technique is to connect thumb to each fingertip in turn, which helps to centre thoughts and emotions. (Using worry beads or hand massage balls can also fight the fidgets.)

Deep breathing is essential to steady nerves. Inhale through your nose while pressing the tongue firmly but without strain on the roof of the mouth. You should feel the expansion of the diaphragm as you do so. Release the tongue and exhale through the mouth.

The following techniques reduce the likelihood of "over breathing" and warm up your voice:

1. Inhale. Exhale … then force-exhale the residual air from your lungs.
2. Bend forward. Breathe in with arms upraised above your head. Expel the air in a long hissing action until your lungs feel quite empty. Your next breath will be easy and natural. This action is useful for getting in touch with the correct mechanism of breathing, noting the action of the muscles of the diaphragm and the lower back, rather than for your actual speaking.
3. Buzz your lips while humming a simple melody or scale.
4. Make rolled "rrr" sounds to loosen your tongue and improve diction.
5. Do the Alexander Technique "whispered ahh" several times. Stand balanced and upright. Smile broadly showing the teeth, which are lightly touching but unclenched. Let your jaw swing open easily while exhaling on a whispered "ahh." This is the purest, uninterrupted sound you can make. It relaxes the jaw, improving projection and tone, frees the crucial neck hinge, opens the important bronchial throat passage, and encourages deep, natural breathing. Benefits include easing tension and nausea and reducing the risk of stuttering and stammering. More oxygen enters the blood stream and senses are heightened.

The minutes before

The territory between your anonymous seat backstage and the brightly lit stage has been called the "launching pad". The moments before launching into a performance can make a crucial difference between maintaining calm control or succumbing to blind panic. You need to learn to slow down while still on the launching pad, to resist the impulse to rush on and tumble headlong into an incoherent presentation.

From the following suggestions assemble your own launch-pad checklist:

1. Sit comfortably, visualise transferring all your nervous energy away from the tense part of your body (e.g. the jaw) down into your toes. Think "toes, toes, toes" and your jaw relaxes.
2. Give your hands about twenty vigorous shakes.
3. Sip some water or rinse your mouth.
4. Think "I feel fine, my fingers and shoulders are relaxed, I am in good form. The audience will like me."
5. Keep thinking positively as the time to take to the stage approaches. Turn down the volume of negative voices in your head. Instead, focus on the outcome you desire – to inspire, to entertain, to "sell", to be invited back.
6. Think through the content you will present. See yourself focused, voice projecting effortlessly and clearly.
7. Let off tension with a silent laugh or sob. Yawn. Stretch. Check your posture by standing against a wall.
8. Bend your knees to unlock tension.
9. Imagine "I am the greatest". Assume a confident, smiling celebrity mood.
10. Slow down.
11. Place a hand on your forehead. Breathe in and out slowly.

Chapter 8

You're on!

Some speakers revel in the sheer buzz and electrical intensity of the adrenaline rush, the stage-lights, and the applause. Others grow to like rather than dread the whole scenario, the more experience they gain.

For those of you who still find it an ordeal, it requires enormous courage to walk on stage and open your mouth. Your stomach is an aviary of butterflies and moths. A compost heap of worms, caterpillars and other greeblies are gnawing at your gut. But somehow you must attach a positive smile to your face or, if your personality prefers, a sober, dignified mien. However, be aware that people do respond to a bright face and especially to a smile. Act, if necessary.

Be prepared for the flow of adrenaline, and welcome it, for it will give energy and strength to your performance, but don't become obsessed about it. Remember, it is a natural, normal and helpful reaction, as long as you don't fight it.

Stand upright, but not ramrod stiff, with shoulders down and chin slightly raised as if looking over the crowd. Walk confidently, but not too quickly, onto the stage. Ah, you hear the applause? Remember, it is just reasonable good manners to acknowledge this with a smile and nod.

Although speakers rarely give a formal bow, it is useful to know how to do it for that particularly illustrious occasion. To bow, look down at your shoes, slowly bending at the hips, count to three, then return to the upright position.

Never, never start with an apology about your lack of experience or poor public speaking track record. Your listeners might well wonder, if you aren't qualified, why are you there?

Take a few moments to poise yourself before starting. These seconds may seem an age to you but they are not to your audience. They capture attention and the atmosphere's spell, quieten the rowdy and establish a calm beginning for yourself. Silence is a potent attention-gatherer.

Where is your audience? If they are huddled at the back of a large auditorium you won't want to bellow to be heard. Overcome any reluctance to move forward by saying: "Would you please all stand. Look at your feet. Now, while you're doing that, move forward to the front rows." They usually will laugh and comply. If presenting an after dinner speech or otherwise competing with cutlery and food, prime the MC to prompt the audience to turn their chairs to face you.

The ensuing shuffle gives you a last chance to open your vocal folds with your silent laugh, with the beginning-yawn or by mouthing the word "one". Focus on projecting the first sentence clearly to ensure free, positive resonance. First impressions linger.

The crucial positive opening

Those first words are vital for your own confidence and the audience's appraisal of you. If your initial sound is squeezed out with strangled tension or a miscalculation of projection, your stomach will plummet. You may think, "Oh, no, this is going to be a fiasco!" (Resist that thought. If this does happen, forge on valiantly; you can still settle down and redeem the performance.)

On the other hand, if that first word sings out beautifully modulated with seemingly effortless ease, your confidence will soar with it. The public speaker must capture the audience in that first tantalising sentence. Many listeners give undivided attention only at the beginning and end of a speech. Choose your opening gambit with care, condensing into it your most arresting statement or an intriguing question, a quotation or startling fact, or a story. People of all ages love stories, but they must be relevant.

Opening with a joke, especially if well chosen and to the point, can be brilliantly effective. However it is not essential, especially if joke telling is contrary to your personal style. If it crashes like a bombed plane, both speaker and listeners may be tempted to go home early. A self-deprecating anecdote usually is better digested than a canned or ancient, recycled joke. Audiences appreciate original humour directed towards oneself, are repelled when it denigrates a defenceless victim.

If your take-off is smooth the rest of the flight usually flows with fewer bumps. Navigate your course with a clear focus on the horizon – your audience – rather than dwell inward on your own queasy stomach and sensitive ego. Most fears are self-centred. Keep looking out!

Most listeners will empathise with your agonies but would prefer not to suffer along with you. They are there to enjoy themselves, to be enlightened, provoked or touched by your content. Rather than wish you ill, they want you to succeed. Adopt a friendly face from the audience and pretend she is your grandmother in whose eyes you can do no wrong. Speak to her.

A less successful ploy is to pretend that the audience is not there, like an ostrich with its head in the sand, or the monkeys who see no evil. This may be a reasonable coping mechanism, but a cough or squirm will soon remind you of their existence. It might result in a bland, acceptable effort, at best.

It is far better to cultivate an attitude of giving to the audience, rather than trying to pretend that they have been magically spirited away. Audiences notice and appreciate this and respond in turn.

Empathy from caring, understanding supporters makes a huge difference to our ability to project and communicate, and, consequently, to relax and perform at our best. Encourage supportive friends and family to attend your presentations by telling them just how much you appreciate their presence.

If you see frowning faces in the audience, have the courage to assume that it is caused by poor indigestion, toothache, a fracas with their partner, or today's letter from the bank manager. Anything other than your own presentation.

Often we imagine criticism where none was intended. It is easy to misread listeners' body language, facial expressions and reactions. On occasion I have been aware and wary of a sober face and assumed they were bored or unimpressed. Inevitably it was those same people who most thanked me, saying how my content had challenged, moved them or given much to absorb. Why do we rush to think the worst?

Tell yourself: "These people have come to hear me, this is a wonderful opportunity to inspire them." As success breeds success, so a positive attitude earns respect.

Actor Ingrid Bergman was depressed by the panel's reactions at her first audition: the jury members were chatting and paying no attention. She went blank with despair. Thinking they didn't think she was worth listening to, she decided life wasn't worth living. She would throw herself in the sea and commit suicide.

Fortunately Bergman decided against this. Years later she asked one of the jury why they disliked her so much. He responded: "Disliked you so much! Dear girl, you're crazy! The minute you leapt out of the wings onto the stage, we turned around and said to each other, 'Well, we don't have to listen to her, she's in!'"

We can become inward and self-centred when panic strikes. Instead of huddling inside our fragile psyches, we need to lift our eyes, to look outside ourselves. As the 17th century Puritan John Bunyan wrote: "Then fancies fly away, I'll fear not what men say."

The eyes have it

The public do respond positively to eye contact. Force yourself to haul your eyes from the floor – a give-away sign of insecurity. Many nervous performers fix their gaze on inanimate objects like the ceiling or a light fitting. As well as alienating the listeners, and giving the performer a glassy, unnatural bearing, this ploy is not usually effective. Experienced speakers who worry about losing their drift if they actually look at the audience, focus just a little above their faces, or at their hairlines.

Stammering and stumbling

Fear of stammering is a major bogey. The average person thinks at the speed of about 700 words per minute, but speaks at 150 to 180 words per minute. No wonder that if nerves paralyse us, while our heartbeat hammers faster, the thinking apparatus and tongue appear to tangle. An ideal rate is an average of 120-150 words per minute. Pause ... breathe out then in, slowly.

Many speakers and actors conquered – or outgrew – stammering. King George VI tried to avoid the throne as he stammered badly; his first radio speech was a fiasco. His wife (the "Queen Mother") encouraged him to work with a Harley Street speech expert, Australian Lionel Logue. He helped the king overcome stutters and face radio microphones to rally his empire to war. With considerable practice, he became fluent and confident.

Another stuttering king, Charles I, avoided the problem altogether. On ascending the British throne in 1623, he merely told Parliament: "I am unfit for speaking" and sat down. King Phillip of Spain had a lisp. Courtiers imitated him to gain favour and so the Spanish pronunciation of "s" became entrenched as "th".

Actor Bruce Willis' stutters disappeared after he joined a high school drama group. Gerard Depardieu was a childhood "dunce" who stammered so badly he could not finish a sentence. Psychological problems locked Depardieu in a nightmare emotional tangle, disrupting his memory and concentration until Dr Alfred Tomatis prescribed daily hours of listening to filtered Mozart and Gregorian chant. Depardieu's mind, speech and concentration were unlocked to reveal extraordinary creative intelligence, near-photographic memory and perfect musical pitch! His many film roles have included acting in a foreign language, English.

The most acclaimed of the ancient Greek orators, Demosthenes, overcame his initial weak voice, poorly constructed sentences and bad stammer. After being ridiculed in an early debate, he locked himself away in his study and practised for weeks. It is said that he cured himself of stammering by practising his speeches with pebbles in his mouth, while walking on the beach at Piraeus. He overcame his shortness of breath by reciting poetry while running uphill. With much practice, his oratory was so renowned that his reputation is prominent thousands of years later.

Renowned Australian actor, John Bell, was heartened by Demosthenes' example. He wrote in his biography *The Time of my Life*: "Another thing that drove me to act was a determination to conquer a frightful stutter. I had begun stammering round about the age of 12; by the time I was 15 I couldn't get a word out without turning crimson, choking and stuttering."

Inspired by Demosthenes' example, he turned to acting as a means of curing his weakness: "So I knew it could be beaten; I would have to beat it by acting in public. It was tough going at first and I often had to change words or ad lib to get through. It took me twenty years to finally master the problem, and even today, when I am tired or overwrought, I get an attack of stammers, but, thankfully, not on stage."

John Bell's long, respected career on the boards started because of an impediment – one which his audiences would be surprised to hear that such a master of language ever experienced.

Marilyn Monroe's signature breathy voice evolved because a speech coach taught her to use exaggerated mouth movements to curb stuttering.

Like shakes, the more you try to control stammers, the more they escalate. If your tongue tangles, stop, have a drink of water and a slow breath. Try reverse psychology. Think: "OK, tongue, just go ahead and trip."

Research suggests that stuttering is caused by the brain's capacity to process speech, rather than a social or psychological disorder. To whisper may reduce stuttering as it is less complex than speaking normally; less auditory feedback is involved. Humming is an excellent way to control breath and speech. A situation can be rescued with a quiet phrase hummed while writing information on a flipchart, passing out handouts or just walking across the platform. Incorporate a song into your speech and the audience will love you!

Frequent sentence fillers like "um" and "er" allow the speaker time to process thoughts but disrupt the flow of speech. Audiences can excuse a few such intrusions. In fact, when some presentations were studio edited of all "um" they lost the sense of natural spontaneity. But excess fillers do distract and many speakers are unaware how often they intrude. Record your presentations periodically and listen back later, when more objective. If you become aware of excess "um" while speaking, create variations with "thus", "on the other hand" or "my point is".

Rather than give yourself mental slaps on the wrist when you notice verbal fillers, turn them into a pause. Silence highlights your next words. Use those vital seconds to think and to take an energising breath. Your voice will project stronger, more resonant – and confident.

The power of the pause

For speakers, silence is also potent. As you stand on the platform, about to speak, WAIT. That pause draws audience attention, quietens the chatterers. To highlight an important point, PAUSE. This gives more potent significance than you would do by than raising your voice and thumping the lectern.

Pause is Politic! French President Francois Mitterrand injected powerful silence into his speeches. In 1974, when in opposition, his speech time consisted of 30% pauses, with an average of 0.8 seconds' silence at ends of sentences. By 1984, at the peak of his popularity, 45% of speech time consisted of pauses, and with 2.1 seconds at ends of his sentences. (Study by Dr Danielle Duez, quoted in "The Best Presentation Skills" by Iain Ewing, 1994)

Audiences appreciate time to absorb our words; we gain breathing space, clarity and poise. Give yourself time and you will speak with confidence!

Avoid death by PowerPoint

"Not another PowerPoint presentation!" audiences groan. This has become addictive for speakers as it allows easy ordering of points and information. But listeners are insulted if the presenter merely reads slides rather than speaking to them or spends much of the time wrestling with the technology. Here are some ways to keep people involved:

"Words, words, words, I'm so sick of words!" exclaimed Henry Higgins in My Fair Lady. Keep each slide's text to a minimum.

Ensure slides are readable by using large font, a minimum of 36 point. Avoid the lower quarter of slide or people at the back of the room will crane to read it – then give up and become restive.

Give them a break; black the screen! Simply press the B key on your laptop and the focus is instantly on you, not the screen. Press B to return.

A picture tells a thousand words but choose illustrations carefully so they enhance your presentation. Clip-art of the fluffy slippers and hair rollers ilk are so yesterday! Instead, add panache and engage listeners' creative right brain hemisphere. Stay within your company format and template but add graphics and contrasting tones that highlight presentations.

Handling mistakes

A few mistakes do not a fiasco make. Professionals throw them off casually but file them away to reinvent as an endearing anecdote in later presentations. Make them part of the performance! Put them behind you and keep going whatever happens. That moment is already passed, you cannot go back in time and fix it.

Flusters over small mishaps of technology or statistics are not important enough to sabotage a whole presentation. Don't look back, or, like Lot's wife, you will be turned into a pillar of salt ... or something equally inanimate and bitter tasting.

If you momentarily lose your train of thought, simply pause. Place a hand on your forehead while you exhale (for, in panic, you probably held your breath) then slowly inhale. Brain fog can happen to anyone. If you don't make a "thing" about it, the audience will either not notice, or will forgive. Mishaps or pauses that seem to be enormous and lengthy to the presenter are usually minuscule in reality.

Where relevant, humour can be a big audience winner. Jokes are safest if turned on oneself, perhaps relating a mishap or embarrassing situation. People respond to your openness. Don't embarrass other people.

Beware especially of racism, profanity, or stamping on religious and political corns. Test those hilarious jokes on the family over breakfast to discover just how effective they are. If you do upset anyone, have the courage and grace to apologise.

How do we give birth to a healthy joke? First don't announce it's on the way! Dress it subtly, let it grow unawares. Curb that expectant grin. Pause for emphasis before the delivery, then wait a moment for listeners to register and laugh. It will be stillborn if you rush on before they have time to react. If a joke does miscarry, carry on regardless.

Watch the clock

Bring a watch or small clock so you can pace your time. Don't rely on finding one at each venue. Start on time and finish on time. Respect your listeners' busy schedules and the next speaker's time limits.

Perhaps you have miscalculated your time, and the master of ceremonies is pointing to his watch. Rather than scramble whole chunks into the last minutes, take a breath while you consider which less important points should be omitted. You might ask the audience which of several items would be most valuable and hint that so much material warrants a return visit! Resist overloading your audience with more information than they can absorb. The old performers' adage "Leave 'em wanting more" is true for speakers.

Be brief. Listeners welcome a punchy, tightly worded, clear speech rather than droning and convoluted mumbling. One does not have to speak long to be remembered; the Sermon on the Mount takes about five minutes to read aloud. Abraham Lincoln's Gettysburg address consists of just 10 sentences.

Expect less time

Much as we time our presentation in advance, often there is less than anticipated. Perhaps the previous speaker ran over-time; the audience is desperate for a coffee break after your presentation, so you won't do the same.

This does not faze you for you have prepared your pre-presentation checklist:
- Rehearse your pithy arresting opening so it's autopilot secure.
- Rehearse your memorable exit lines (e.g. a call to action).
- Plan which aspects are priority and which can be dropped if necessary.
- Plan a quick segue if you have to cut to the conclusion sooner.

The conclusion

Foolproof phrases to rouse flagging interest begin "Finally ...", "To sum up ..." or "Let me stress ..." This directs back any wandering attentions to focus on your last minutes.

Put as much thought into your last sentence as you did your first. You want the audience to take away the essence of your speech. Leave them with the sense that the time they have spent listening to you has been worthwhile. Perhaps they feel uplifted, challenged or fired for action. Or more relaxed after enjoying your company, your wit and humour.

There are many ways to cross the finishing line. You may encapsulate your content with a quotation or joke that will leave them on a high note. Briefly summarise your main points, or answer a question raised at the outset. Offer a solution to a problem or some satisfying conclusion so the audience feels they have gained from hearing you. Signal finality by slowing the pace towards the end and look directly at your listeners to give strength and intensity to your last words.

People love to receive something extra, free of charge. Handouts or a well-chosen small gift which reminds them of your central message can be given at the end of your presentation rather than earlier when this would distract from your spoken words.

Question time

"What will they ask me?" The fear of the unknown causes many novice speakers to flinch at the thought of answering questions. You will not have this worry if your speech preparation included noting potential queries and practice of appropriate answers.

The words "Are there any questions?" often are met with bald silence. This does not imply failure. If your presentation was so concise and clear that no clarification is needed, or the audience needs a break after a long presentation, don't extract unwilling questions. Many people may be shy of speaking out and prodding is counterproductive.

Perhaps you might plant a colleague in the audience, primed with a preferred question which you can answer with ease. This breaks that uneasy ice and triggers other questions. Or you could clear the fog with: "Often I'm asked …"

Because listeners use a different part of the brain when absorbing content, they may be not yet ready to verbalise. A less threatening prompt is to ask them to "Turn to the person next to you and discuss if you have any questions that need clarification." Or you might casually say, "While I drink a glass of water, think if you have any questions to ask me." That water will also help you to think fast if any curly questions are lobbed from left field! In which case, pause. Reflect. (Perhaps during that moment, ask if a member of the audience may answer the question for you.)

Repeat each question, not only for the people at the back of the hall – who will appreciate your consideration – but also for the tape if you have agreed to a recording. Rephrase and simplify any convoluted or stumbling questions.

Remember, you are the expert. You were invited to speak because of acknowledged qualification or experience. You are prepared, up to date on the research. Most of the audience could not match your command of the topic. Although some questions may be tricky, delivered from grandstands or pushed in wheelbarrows, it is rare that they are actually as hostile as they might first seem. An "on-edge" presenter may misread an enthusiastic question as an effort to trip him or her.

Compliment useful or stimulating queries to reinforce important points from your presentation: "That's an excellent question, I'm glad you raised it." (But don't enthuse over all questions or you may appear fawning.) Phrases like "As you no doubt know …" "Perhaps you might briefly share your expertise with us …" defer to their knowledge while giving yourself time to marshal your own thoughts. Remember, you are the expert, the floor is yours. You own the space.

If relevant slides would complement your answer, the Macintosh

"View presenter tools" allows speakers to scroll to a relevant slide or by typing in the number of the slide (25 return – or enter for PC). Write on a card slide numbers for section changes. Note must-hear points and your final slide. You could print out the notes pages, but a small card is more accessible.

If you cannot answer a question, it is better to admit it openly than to tangle yourself up in convoluted attempts. People appreciate the honesty of "I don't think I could do justice to that complicated question without further time or research, but I would be happy to follow it up with you later." Or "I am not prepared to answer that at present; would someone else like to enlarge on it?"

Perhaps you might feel challenged of neglecting certain sources or accused of omitting important points. Check that you understand each other before hackles rise. They may be working on similar research. Look for areas on which you can agree.

In the unlikely event that you do encounter open hostility, drop your shoulders, take a deep breath and a drink of water. Listen carefully to their points, looking to agree on some common ground. Empathy helps to defuse possible aggression and maintains rapport with the rest of the audience.

Remain objective and realise the person may be envious of your position on the podium. Understanding their position enables you to respond with compassion. Maintain a neutral, even voice and avoid emotive language. Look on this as an excellent opportunity to re-state your position: "Let me clarify my point." Find a source of agreement: "I understand that you do agree with me on ..." Or cut it short with "I value your question but I don't think it's applicable to today's topic. I'm happy to discuss it further if you come and see me later."

If you do feel threatened, deal with their point briefly and then call for the next question. Dodge inelegant public power-struggles that will alienate the rest of the audience, who are otherwise on your side. Most grandstanders will desist once they have their quota of attention. If they try to turn it into a debate, suggest following up the discussion at the end of the session rather than take time from others' questions.

Keep an eye on the time so your audience does not become restive. Give a brief wrap-up, restate your conclusion and thank them for their interest.

After the applause

This book has shown how you can turn those negatives that formerly blocked you into positives that allow your imagination to blossom, your sentences to flow, your words to soar. Now, instead of being knocked sideways by the wave of adrenaline, you can understand and anticipate, utilise, and even welcome it. Properly channelled, this adrenaline will lift that performance from the merely mundane to an exciting and enriching event.

A majority of people struggle through life without ever confronting their worst fears. You are amongst the minority of courageous survivors for you have looked your demons squarely in the face. Congratulations.

You have suppressed unnecessary excesses of ego to the validity of your message and your listeners' needs. You have met the "enemies" and discovered that they are your friends.

Communication is a two-way equation and your audience relates to how you see them. Now, by throwing off your defences you can build an affinity with your listeners as living, breathing people, instead of a sea of eyes. They will respond as you send out positives with love and humour and you will enjoy your time on the platform.

What you give out comes back to you. If the presenter is positive, at ease, happy, so is the audience. Importantly, so is the person who pays your fee, who might invite you to return! There is some truth in that old joke: "Do I have to inject humour into a speech?" "Only if you want to be paid."

Now, as you square your shoulders, breathe, smile and walk on stage to confront those glinting sabre-toothed tigers' eyes, you will discover instead beautiful, soft, friendly pussycats. Hear them purr, as they applaud your words.

You can now take centre-stage with confidence and enjoy your time in the warm glow of the spotlights. Be yourself. Give out. Enjoy!

"Bravo!"

Further reading and bibliography

The following books have been referred to and in some cases briefly quoted from:

Barlow, Wilfred, *The Alexander Principle: How to Use Your Body* (Arrow Books, London, 1975)

Bergman, Ingrid and Alan Burgess, *Ingrid Bergman: My story* (Sphere Ltd., London, 1972)

Bryant, Chris, *Glenda Jackson, The Biography* (HarperCollins, 2000)

Bell, John, *The Time of my Life* (Allen and Unwin, 2002)

Campbell, Don, *The Mozart Effect* (Hodder and Stoughton, 1997)

Chutkow, Paul, *Gerard Depardieu: A Biography*, (HarperCollins 1994)

Chopra, Depak, *Perfect Health* (Bantam Books, NY, 1990)

Cousins, Norman, *Anatomy of an Illness* (Norton, NY, 1979)

Dennison, Paul E. and Gail E. Dennison *Brain Gym: Teachers' Edition* (Edu-Kinesthetics Inc., California, 1989 and 1994)

Freeman, Walter J., *How Brains Make Up their Minds* (Phoenix, London, 1999)

Gelb, Michael, *Present Yourself* (Aurum Press, London, 1988)

Hannaford, Carla, *Smart Moves: Why learning is not all in your head* (Great Ocean, Arlington, Virginia, 1995)

Krebs, Dr Michael, *A Revolutionary Way of Thinking* (Hill of Content, 1998, Melbourne)

McCallion, Michael, *The Voice Book* (Faber, London, 1988)

McGraw, Nanci, *Speak Up and Stand Out* (SkillPath Publications, Mission, KS, 1997)

Mehrabian, Albert, 'Significance of Posture and Position in the Communication of Attitude and Status Relationships,' *Psychological Bulletin* 71 (1969), pp. 359-372.

Pease, Allan, *Body Language: How to read others' thoughts by their gestures* (Camel Publishing Company, 1981, 1987)

Tomatis, Alfred A. *The Conscious Ear: My life of transformation through listening* (Station Hill Press, Barrytown, NY, 1991) www.tomatis.com

Web sites:

Information for speakers and singers about voice aspects (speech, twang, falsetto, sob/cry, opera and belting) at Jo Estill's http://thesingingvoice.com/html/joestill.html

Alexander technique: www.alexandertechnique.com

Dr Bach Rescue remedy: http://http://www.bachflower.com/rescue-remedy-information/

Emotional Freedom Technique: http://www.emofree.com/ Article by Ruth Bonetti: http://www.emofree.com/Performance/music-performance-jitters.htm

Index

A

adrenaline 1, 2, 3, 6, 8, 10, 11, 18, 42, 56, 62, 75
Alexander Technique 25, 26, 59
Aristotle 14
audience iv, 3, 10, 13, 25, 33, 34, 38, 47, 52, 53, 57, 60, 63, 64, 65, 66, 68, 70, 71, 72, 73, 74, 75
Aurelius, Marcus 14

B

Bell, John 67
Bergman, Ingrid 65
blood flow 10, 13, 16, 41
Book of Lists 6
Book of Proverbs 12
Brain-Gym 16, 19, 35
breath 8, 15, 18, 20-26, 36-38, 42, 54, 59, 60, 66, 67, 68, 70, 71, 74, 75
Buddha 12, 14
Bunyan, John 66

C

cerebral cortex 15
Chopra, Debra 19
Churchill, Sir Winston 1, 5, 46, 48
Clinton, Bill 36
Cousins, Norman 12
cross-crawl 17, 58

D

Demosthenes 67
Dennison, Paul E and Gail 17, 78
Depardieu, Gerard 67
diarrhoea 9, 40, 42, 53
Diet 30
Disraeli, Benjamin 32

Dr Bach, Rescue Remedy 49, 54
dry mouth 42

E

Emotional Freedom Technique 20
Epictetus 14

F

fight or flight 9, 11, 15, 16, 20, 22, 24, 26, 30
Ford, Henry 14

G

Ghandi, Indira 32

H

Hannaford, Carla 27, 79
heart rate 10, 41, 42, 66
Hoffman, Dustin 1, 15

J

Jackson, Glenda 5, 78

K

Keleman, Stanley 19
Kelly, Grace 32
Kidman, Nicole 1
Kinesiology 16, 19
King George VI 66
King, Martin Luther 1

L

Laryngitis, voice problems 40
Lincoln, Abraham 71

M

McCutcheon, Sandy 57
Mead, Margaret 14
Moses 3, 4, 5

N

nausea 54, 59
Newman, Paul 39

O

Olivier, Sir Laurence 5
Oral twang 38

P

PACE sequence 58
Peale, Norman Vincent 14
Pfeiffer, Michelle 32
Positive Points 16
posture 11, 12, 20, 24, 25, 26, 28, 29, 44, 60
Psychology Today 6

Q

questions 72-75

S

Seinfeld, Jerry 3
self-sabotage 19, 52
Sellers, Peter 1
Sermon on the Mount 71
shakes 60, 68
stammer 9, 67
Streep, Meryl 10
stutter 53, 67
Sweaty hands, perspiration 8

T

Thatcher, Margaret 32
Thornton, Sigrid 54
Tomatis, Dr. Alfred 67

V

Virgil 15
vocal folds 21, 22, 33, 34, 37, 39, 41, 42, 63
Voice warm-up 34, 36

W

water 7, 17, 18, 30, 39, 40, 41, 42, 49, 53, 54, 55, 56, 57, 60, 68, 73, 74
Whispered "ahh" technique 59
Willis, Bruce 67

Y

yawn 22, 33, 34, 35, 56, 63

About the author

Ruth Bonetti applies to speaking platform skills learned in her primary career as a professional musician. Her popular clarinet method *Enjoy Playing the Clarinet* (Oxford University Press) is an international best seller. Ruth's other books have been published by Albatross Books (*Taking Centre Stage*), music syllabus grade books (Allans Publishing) and books to enhance performance published by Words and Music.

Her articles have appeared in print media in Britain, USA and Australia, including Women's Network Magazine, The Australian, The Courier-Mail, The Sunday Mail, and numerous international music journals.

Ruth is an M.Mus performance graduate from University of Queensland. She was a faculty member of Griffith University, Queensland Conservatorium of Music for 15 years and has taught extensively in Australia, Britain, Germany, Sweden and France.

Ruth's music and speaking career has taken her around Australia, Europe and the USA, with recent tours to New Zealand, Germany and Finland, and across Australia from Darwin to Melbourne to Perth. She presents workshops for schools, universities and businesses, developing confident presentation for those who perform via words or music.

www.ingramcontent.com/pod-product-compliance
Lightning Source LLC
Chambersburg PA
CBHW072017290426
44109CB00018B/2265